Beyond Damage

By Julia Kathleen Gillis

Paperback IBSN 978-1-7770106-1-4
Electronic Book IBSN 978-1-7770106-0-7

FIRST EDITION

www.prettyaggressive.com

Cover art generously designed by Adam McCarthy
www.amccarthyfineart.com   & @ac_mccarthy

<u>The Disclaimer</u>

This is the disclaimer: Your mother might not be toxic. Your mother might not be a narcissist, might not be emotionally abusive, might not be unloving. It's possible that she is just really annoying. Or selfish. Or exhausted. Or you have anger from somewhere else and you have chosen her as your target. There is an entire chapter in this book that offers the tool of learning how to not blame your mom (or other people in general.)

But: if your mother has a collection of behaviors and characteristics that are extremely hurtful to you and others - it's probably because she is struggling with a cyclical legacy of pain, passed on to her before you were even born.

Focus on this idea: regardless of who your mother is and how she raised you or treated you growing up or how she treats you now - it is most likely that she was/is only offering what she is capable of. No PERSON has the ability to be everything you need or want them to be. That includes your mother. You're not perfect. She's not perfect. This book is not about villainizing your mother. The purpose of this book is NOT to demonize (or diagnose) your mother, or any other mothers. This book is about you. This book is about who you can be or could be - if you choose.

This book is about learning to thrive.

Because simply surviving - is bullshit.

Take chances! Make Mistakes!
Lets get messy!

- Miss Frizzle, The Magic School Bus

Table of Contents

Introduction

The Goal of this Book

Moving from Surviving to Thriving.
Moving from Survivor to Thriver.

This is now Your Goal. I'm gifting it to you. You can have it.

This book is directed at women who are surviving after living through (or are still currently living with) a mother who is toxic.

Current abuse victims are 'surviving.' In a victimized situation we are stuck in a reptilian mindset. One that is in a constant and toxic infinity loop of shock & reaction. The next level up from this is leaving behind the label of a victim and being reborn as a survivor. This is a recovery and healing period after we have ended or removed ourselves from abuse and trauma. This is a great step to take for personal empowerment. This is an incredible identity that has changed how we are able to cope with shame & pain associated with abuse and trauma. Now I feel it's time that our culture begins offering a place, an idea, a concept beyond this.

There needs to be a new way to look at the work we do on ourselves, that is viewed as more than recovery. We need to set our sights on what we can accomplish beyond healing and repairing damage. There needs to be hope for continued and additional development after this stage.

We also need to leave behind that expectation and stigma of being 'completely healed' before we are able to progress. Who or what determines when we have repaired or recovered 'enough' to title ourselves just a 'person'? It is not easy to grant one's self permission or liberty to claim complete restoration from past grievances. Especially - because as fluid, ever changing humans - this is not possible.

This becomes our cage. A holding pattern. This can forever drown someone working to recover from abuse and trauma. After moving past victimhood, we are imprisoned as a survivor; unable to shake that label. Believing there is no identity for us beyond this.

There is a way for us to build ourselves beyond and above our current framework. We need to believe our shell has potential to expand, to accommodate an excess of progress. We can surpass or transcend our current psychological/mental/emotional domains.

The people in this world who enter the 'thriving' mindset are people who are living beyond trauma, damage, abuse, suffering and victimhood.

My goal is to help you get on with it. Get on with your life. Get on with who you're going to be tomorrow. Get on with who you want to be. Not get over it. You will learn that this is an anti-concept. There is nothing for you to 'get over' because how you were raised is not an obstacle for you to wrestle with in order to become the person you want to be. Waiting to repair yourself, waiting to fully recover can smother or snuff out the hope of being a person beyond your damage. You don't need to be 'perfect' in the present to work at your future self.

The pieces of you that are uncomfortable, that hurt, the pieces you hide - you needn't banish them. Allow them a piece of your attention. Tend to your wounds with patience and acceptance. Busy the rest of yourself with growth. Acknowledge your strengths and celebrate them by using them. Win, rest, fail, and learn to laugh at yourself.

A thriver accepts the gradient. In life, and within themselves. A thriver embraces the imperfection of 'self.' A thriver can conceive of being more than an accumulation of their current parts. A thriver creates a path in front of themselves based on where they want to go; not where they have been.

Live beyond your toxic parents' trauma & pain.

Live beyond your own labels and lies.

Live beyond the damage.

You are more than that. You are greater than that.

<u>Chapter 1</u>
Before you get into this book, make sure it's for you.

This book is for women who are searching for recovery from unloving mothers. This book is both a memoir and a self help book. It's also an aggressive learning curve. It began as a tool for myself, and morphed into a desire to help others, due to the lack of effective solutions I was finding in the related literature. I'm going to share with you my journey to a better life - a life I found beyond my mother and beyond my damage; but no longer beyond my control.

Most important: I'm going to share the most effective tools I have come up with to rewire the brain after being raised by a mother who doesn't know how to love. At the beginning of my journey to find recovery, I came across a very informative literary niche. One for daughters struggling with the realization that the root of their persistent life problems was the poorly bonded (read: emotionally abusive) mothering they received. Within this niche I found massive insight, but struggled to apply many of the recovery tools presented. I found these books out of my desperation to heal. I wanted tools for changing how I think & behave, how I see the world & myself and exercises I could use when I find myself dragged back into old habits. Instead, I more often found clinical descriptions of emotionally abusive parenting, related insight, a slew of triggering traumatic stories and endless reminders of how that damage plays out into adulthood.

This book is for women that understand who they are, have a 'good enough' understanding of their mother's tortured soul and are ready to:

Move

- The Fuck -

On.

We will not be opening our hearts to the universe. I will not be guiding you through living with better gratitude from a place of love. I will not be helping you 'consider' becoming more open minded to concepts like meditation. I will not be offering warm, fuzzy things so you can gently approach a more inclusive and holistic experience on our physical plain. We will not be learning to vibrate at a higher frequency.

This book is a Louisville slugger to a set of headlights. This book is the shove. It's the push. This book is not a path - it's an uphill, rugged, unmarked cliffside.

Beyond Damage - Julia Gillis - 2019

This book's focus is not for developing self awareness.
Our focus is changing the self you are already aware of.

If you had a neglectful, emotionally abusive, gaslighting, narcissistic or toxic mother, you have very specific traits. Some of them are horrible. But oddly some of those traits are extremely impressive to others. Some of them are also the traits that help you survive. Unfortunately we never feel that way about ourselves. No matter how much other people tell us. This needs to stop.

Before reading this book, make sure you have a relatively good understanding of the 'type' of unloving mother you had and the subsequent issues you have developed from that. If this is the first book on the topic you have come across and need a more detailed background on your mother and yourself, I would suggest some of the following books.

- *Will I Ever Be Good Enough* by Karyl McBride, Ph. D
- *Mothers Who Can't Love* by Susan Forward, Ph. D
- *The Emotionally Absent Mother* by Jasmin Lee Cori, MS. LPC
- *Daughter Detox* by Peg Streep
- *Mean Mothers* by Peg Streep
- *Toxic Parents* by Susan Forward
- *Adult Children of Emotionally Immature Parents* by Lindsay C. Gibson, PsyD

If you have not come across or read any of these books, I have a few cautionary comments:

1. I would suggest picking one of the Ph.D authors and one Peg Streep book and crushing them. Then come back to this one.

2. Don't spend more than 2-3 days with each of these books; they can be very triggering. When in a dark, self deprecating place, the tools can be difficult to find and apply properly.

3. Also look into the laundry list for Adult Children of Alcoholics. The same traits can be found in just about any adult child of an abusive parent, including narcissistic parents.

These books, explain the different ways your mom is screwed up, and the different ways you're screwed up. It goes into depth explaining different types of horrible mothers and sheds light on why she is probably that way. They share stories throughout, that you can't avoid, from other women with relatable feelings and moments that can trigger you into a dark place and drag you into a hole. They often spend only the last 10-30% of the book offering tools for healing which range from slightly helpful to archaic, awkward, Freudian, and at times, misdirected and useless.

I have read these books, I have dug up the memories, I have dragged myself into the mud, ended up living there for a while, and then become disgusted with myself. But like many daughters of an unloving mother, failure isn't an option. Even if you're told (or it's insinuated) you are one, and always will be, and that you're designed that way.

You also don't have time to buy a crib, put it in a special room and pretend to parent your invisible, imaginary childhood self. That is for crazy people; and we are here because we don't want to be one anymore.

You're also sick of the following things:
1) going to therapy that doesn't seem to have a finish line
2) feeling sorry for yourself
3) pulling yourself to pieces and being depressed for weeks at a time
4) Self-sabotaging your relationships, opportunities and life in general
5) having disturbing memories on repeat in your head like a instagram gif

Last but not least, you're probably sick of your mother.

There are a number of other books I **do** recommend you read, listed in Chapter 5. Which I have read or listened to on audio multiple times. Sometimes even multiple times in a row. Which I found powerfully positive and helpful.

If you, for any reason, need a recap on narcissism, malignant narcissism, emotional abuse styles, bad mothering types, gaslighting and all the number of horrible attributes these things develop into when you're parented with them, feel free to turn to the very back of the book. I've created cliff notes for easy reference.

Our goal is to make sure you've left the place of 'victim' behind you. We are going to remove that description from your identity. On top of that - we're going to change you from 'survivor' to 'thriver.' Tough concept; I know. But it's real and we can do it.

If you're ready for tools that will help you change the parts of yourself that are holding you back from being a better person & you are ready to have a better life despite the damaging ways your mother raised you - read on. This book is your gateway to finally Thrive.

There is a life beyond your damage.

Chapter 2
Fluid Acceptance;
The Foundation of Your Change.

Have you read a bunch of books on unloving mothers? Have you google searched your neurosis to death? Do you know all the clinical explanations related to your issues? Have you uncovered the life web that puts rhyme and reason behind your toxic relationship with your mother (and yourself)? What happens when you have explored the therapy techniques, unmailed letter writing, inner child comforting, pillow punching, and meditation energy healing exercises? You've uncovered everything. You are at the bottom of an empty Felix the Cat bag.

This book is for women in that place. It is for women who have done everything they can but don't feel like they've healed. You're not 'done.'

You know there must be an answer.

Logical, pragmatic, effective solutions.

Spelled out clearly.

That don't feel ridiculous. And Freudian. This is THE book. This book has real tools for real women, who really want to get better. I did the work, I found the tools. Every woman who is suffering from a childhood without a loving mother should be offered these tools. There are some significant differences between this book and other books on healing from mothers who can't love. All of the descriptions you've come across that explain the different types of abusive mothers, the clinical trials with mothers and babies and what they tell us about bonding, the results of neglect, gaslighting, pitting siblings against each other, and endless examples of fucked up internal behavior that you relate to; that is at the very back of this book. It is in short form and should only be referred to if necessary. You will not find excerpts of other women's unhappy (read: shitty) relationships with their mothers and their epiphany moments, or reflections of these, spread throughout this book. You will find my tortured memories compiled in one place, in a single chapter, after the tools for healing. And you are welcome to skip it. It is not required reading.

Now I'm going to tell you something harsh: you will never be done healing. These books and therapists and experts that offer you exercises and ways to heal, they aren't misleading you - but they fail to emphasize something really important:

You will not ever finish 'healing' or getting better or getting over it.

That's not a place for you to get to. Do you know what that place is? Perfection. It's Utopia. Atlantis. And it's not a real place. It's this fictional, far off land created for people who have endless money to waste on the products & services that make them feel like one day - they could be the next Buddha.

That's not real.
>   **Let that idea go.**
>>   **Right now.**

You will not ever finish that last book, or have that last therapy session and look in the rear view mirror to find all of your painful memories sorted out into cute little boxes, with labels that explain or justify everything. You will not find your childhood self sitting around smiling and waving; so glad that you went back and parented them yourself with the love and kindness you missed out on. Sorry.

But this is the point. You will never be perfect; and that is very, very, **very** ok. It's more than ok. You shouldn't be perfect. It's exhausting and gross. And it will turn you into the mother you hated. The most comfortable place for you to get, while working through your childhood trauma, abuse, pain, suffering, etc... is a place of fluidity.

This is actually where healthy, well bonded, secure people live. They live in a world where it's ok to not be perfect. They see themselves as a human, with the normal human condition of having positive attributes as well as an acceptable amount of attributes that require development and work. No one ever suggested, insinuated or stated that perfection was a place for them to aspire to. They live in a mindset where, throughout their life, mistakes will be made, they will learn from them, and grow. Then they will do it all over again.

Mistake, learn, grow. Repeat.

Also, regardless of which section of that process they are in...they still have an adequate amount of self worth. You can find a way to live in this mindset too.

This is the foundation tool you will need to get better. Not get over it. Not heal. Not find inner peace. Just better. This foundation tool needs to be used in conjunction with the other tools I share in this book, that you will need to use for the rest of your life. This first tool I share, will also help you understand 'why' it requires continued use.

I use a term called **Fluid Acceptance.**

What I've learned through this process of battling my inner demons is that believing you can eventually lay them to rest is a fictional, disappointing, futile struggle. It's as pointless as trying to please your narcissistic mother. As pointless as your fight to experience her unconditional love. But accepting defeat is not the answer either. That is the other extreme that isn't fair. Fluid acceptance is about getting comfortable in the gray zone; it's about living in a gradient. You neither have to aim for that place where you are 'fixed,' nor do you have to succumb to being 'broken.'

Some women want to finally let go of their mothers, some want to forgive them, some want to find inner peace after getting past the pain. There came a point in my path where I discovered those goals aren't realistic. (Also the focus is in the wrong place.) Even when people claim they have done this - I feel they are lying to themselves if they don't admit they still have hard days. Everyone regresses at some point. Old emotions can get triggered and rise up. The truth is: there is a back and forth. They can't all be good days. But you can change how you feel & cope with your 'bad' days. So let's call it what it is and not feign ultimate success. Lets not glamourize this and tell people they can get to a perpetual place of peace.

Our particular upbringing causes us to have a hard time accepting the fluidity of the human condition. We live in a constant and hardlined dichotomy. Two realities seem to exist for us at all times. We believe we should be perfect and that no one will love us or accept us if they see or realize that we aren't. But for some reason we are able to watch everyone else not be perfect. We watch them have relationships and be loved and fuck up, only to get back up and carry on. Their world doesn't end or shatter.

A good human is never done working on themselves or done attempting to be better. As a daughter of an unloving, emotionally abusive or narcissistic mother... your wounds are deep and your upbringing has hardwired you to malfunction. Even when you are done uncrossing a bunch of those wires, and those scabs have healed, your brain will still have sockets with burn marks that you can't scrub off and your scars will still catch in the sunlight on your skin.

That is Nothing To Be Ashamed Of.

You are coloured by your past. Your resiliency and tenacity is what makes you the incredible person you are. Flaws, foibles, quirks and fuck ups. Embrace the nature of forever growing. Which means the person you were yesterday, wasn't as smart or capable as you are today. And today, you're more of a screw up than you will be tomorrow after you learn today's lessons. Which isn't horrible. It's amazing! Fluid acceptance.

REWIRE YOUR BRAIN

Recap: When you have an unloving mother you develop a number of parallel realities. The most significant one being that you are suppose to be perfect in order to be loved. While knowing, at the exact same time, no one is subject to this requirement. You watch everyone else walking around, not being perfect. You even see the imperfections in your loved ones and keep loving them. But you can't comprehend the scenario of having anyone find out that you aren't perfect, or fail sometimes - and still keep their love. That just can't be possible!

News flash.
They already know you aren't perfect.
You're not fooling anyone.
Already.
The jig was up a long time ago.

How to start uncrossing those wires: This is a step by step process to start gaining fluid acceptance and live in that mindset as often as possible. You don't necessarily have to do it in this order. But you need to do this constantly. All the time. Until it becomes habitual.

1. Instead of comparing yourself to others, start grouping yourself with them, specifically in regards to not being perfect. "Other people aren't perfect. No one is perfect. <u>That means me too</u>." Use it all over the place:
    a. People are late sometimes. I was late, just like other people have been before. That's ok.
    b. I expressed extreme emotion. Other people do that. Its ok to express myself openly, just like other people do sometimes.
    c. Everyone needs help when they take on too much at once. Just like me. I need help sometimes and sometimes I can have too much on my plate to handle. That can happen to anyone.
    d. Everyone heals at a different rate. People will heal faster than me. Some will heal slower. I will heal at my own rate, just like everyone.

2. Find a different word other than 'perfect' as a measurement. I spent some time using the mantra "I'm not perfect." It was meant to calm me and remind myself that it was ok to be flawed or make mistakes. But this statement is being used as a reply to something. Why did you forget? Why didn't you succeed? Why did you react so poorly? Because I'm not perfect. Ok. No one is. That statement isn't quantifiable. It is utterly useless at communicating anything helpful. You may as well say "I'm not a unicorn." Throw the word 'perfect' in the garbage. It's the degrading and torturous concept your mother uses to make you feel like shit. Let. It. Go.

3. Find a mantra that does work.
   a. It's ok to make mistakes.
   b. That's the response I chose to go with at the time.
   c. Failing at one or a few things doesn't make me a failure.
   d. If this doesn't work, I can try again.
   e. I can fix this or apologize.
   f. That was an honest reaction.
   g. I just need practice.
   h. I could use some extra help with this.

All of these statements are real, true, applicable and supported by human nature and history.

After this section there will be a number of other tools to use on top of this baseline. You will find these starting in chapter 4.

Never stop applying the concept of fluid acceptance.

Live in the grey zone.
Own the grey zone.

Make the grey zone your bitch.

You are impressive. You are successful at tons of things. You boss your life. Often. But not always. And the moments, days, even weeks, that you don't - are normal. Its ok. The healthy people in your life will still love you. Admit that things aren't going well, take a deep breath, KNOW that this is ok. Then apply the next tool.

Chapter 3
Qualifications, The Rabbit Hole
& Life Beyond Mother

This is where I offer you a story. One that doesn't have an ending, but is going extremely well. As any smart woman should, you will probably ask: What qualifies Julia to offer advice on surviving and thriving after a narcissistic gaslighting mother? I'll tell you my background qualifications:

I have one. A mother I would (unprofessionally) categorize as a gaslighting, malignant narcissist. And I think I'm doing ...pretty well. Better than I've ever been, actually. I've gone through the process of recognizing her for what she is. Then cutting her out of my life. Then pressing hard to uncover, battle and tame the demons she raised me to have. In other words, I've been through the following:

- Feeling unloved by my mother
- Feeling unlovable to others
- Feeling years of shame & insecurity for being inadequate, broken, damaged or not good enough
- Self sabotage, self hate, low self worth and accepting less than I deserve (in many regards)
- Looking back on years of failure, while others only see achievement and strength
- Attending therapy on and off throughout my life for various circumstances that I had no tools for
- Being in a constant merry-go-round of fighting with my mum, apologizing, making up, fighting again, etc
- Hating my mother and having no idea why
- Being made to feel ashamed for being angry with my mother
- Trying to cut my mother out of my life (multiple times)
- Being convinced that this is unacceptable behavior
- Cutting my mother out for the final time
- Having my family disapprove of this choice
- Identifying my mother as a gaslighting, malignant narcissist
- Doing extensive research on both gaslighting & narcissism
- Going to therapy specifically to heal from this

- Being continually harassed by my mother to the point of exploring a restraining order
- Reading multiple books by reputable psychologists on the topic of emotionally absent mothers
- Identifying the problems I have because of how she raised me
- Continually working to accept responsibility for these parts of me
- Continually working to change these parts of me

And now, finally:
- Having a life where I feel proud of who I am & what I'm doing.
- Feeling confident in my choices and my ability to achieve goals I set.
- Feeling more than good enough; for anything I choose.
- Feeling like it's not unreasonable (read: crazy) to insist on being loved in a healthy and supportive way.
- Having confidence in my boundaries, and strength to fight for them when someone else treats them with disrespect.
- Having found some fluid acceptance for my mother's inability to be a warm loving person. I'm not ok with it. I haven't fully forgiven her. But I understand it. And that's enough for me. That can be enough for me to move on and live my life.

Put 'most of the time' at the end of all of these statements. That's where most people live. Again - fluidity.

In addition to this, I have created a tribe of women in my life that are supportive, genuine, compassionate and trustworthy. I can call on these women when I need something. Anything. They can also call on me. We continually build and work on our bonds together. We offer each other the community connection so deeply needed by women, on a biological level.

I'm going to share what I went through, what I figured out, how I got to where I am now and where I plan on going still. When I started writing it was for my own release. But at low moments during my early recovery, I found myself going back to my own writing to analyse memories and dissect experiences I was having and recording. I began finding things that helped me, resparked my drive to get better and keep working on myself. So I started to develop a way to share that with other women that might be struggling. If you can use it and it helps you - that makes me extremely happy. If not, I hope you carry on to find what you're looking for.

The basis of this book is my process to heal (as well as anyone can) from being raised by a mother that I believe is a malignant narcissist and used gaslighting as her defense (read: abuse) tactic. I began writing this book at the end of June 2018. I learned the term 'gaslighting' in October the previous year. I had a rabbit hole experience. The following months were heavy with confusion, loss of my identity, cyclical depression, helplessness, frustration, indignation and rage.

So. Much. Rage.

I felt I had been stripped in public. I can look back at the 24-48 hour time frame that I put the pieces together and just, as some would say, lost my shit.

I'm not sure if I got lucky. After struggling for so many years in my relationship with my mother, and life in general, I'm not confident in using the word luck to explain the realization of my childhood (and adult) emotional abuse. I happened upon something unexpected and very necessary in my search for answers. I think that rarely happens for people. It's that charming moment in every episode of your favorite tv crime show where that final clue is uncovered. Its that slow build of tension, almost to the point of giving up and all of a sudden "Aha!"

But that's a tv show. That's not real life. In real life: it's shocking. And fucking horrifying.

One of the harshest qualities of gaslighting as an abuse style is how insidious it is. It's not in your face like being told you're worthless or that you're a piece of shit. It's not a punch in the face or a shove into a wall. It's not even like being locked in a cupboard for so long you have no choice but to soil yourself. Then yelled at or punished further for that. It's insinuated, it's subtle, it's a chess game you don't even know you're playing. It's just whispers... that no one else can hear. And you question whether you heard them yourself. It was tough to get to the age of 28 and never have heard the term before. I was educated, well read and had received compliments on my level of 'emotional intelligence' since I was young. I also placed myself in the labeled box of having a 'good/normal' family. None of us were 'fucked up.' Except me, really. I was the black sheep. I drank heavily, smoked, had sex too early, got in tons of trouble, ran away (multiple times.) But I was the odd one out. The rest of my family was straight edge and high achieving. Child abuse or abusive relationships weren't 'a thing.' Not even in my extended family. The only person in my house that yelled while I was growing up....was me.

(I later discovered this was completely untrue. The amount of emotional abuse that went on in my family between the generations was excessive. But everyone kept it extremely well hidden. My maternal grandmother raised 5 kids on her own. She was AWFUL to them. Seriously horrendous. Four of those five children went on to have their own children - me, my siblings and my 7 cousins. Turns out we all had problems. The problems didn't start with my grandmother, but she sure as hell gifted them to her kids...and her kids gifted them to us in spades. Our middle to upper-middle class, white, educated, liberal family. The emotionally abusive relationships and events that I explained to my therapist caused him to comment that he's only ever seen such twisted abuse in

Indigenous families. Residential school forced, genocide victim, culturally robbed, poverty stricken, intergenerational drug and alcohol dependant Natives. That was the level of emotional abuse going on in my family. I was so fucking uncomfortable.)

The Rabbit Hole

The blip in time that is the foundation work for wrestling out of my mother's abusive chokehold still shakes me significantly. I look back at it like I imagine an astronaut looks back at the rocket launch site, while floating in space. The final place they touched the earth; before literally becoming a galactic explorer. Leaving the earth's surface is both frightening beyond belief and fucking hurts as you're forced through the atmosphere. Yet at the same time it's the most exhilarating point in your life as you realize you're being shot into the Great Unknown. What is ahead of you is incomprehensible but the feeling to press forward is too exciting for words. Sometimes you realize you're actually flying. Sometimes you realize you're seriously alone and might die randomly. Then, for short periods of time you're able to have some perspective that you've accomplished something incredible - and very necessary.

That is how I felt when I finally decided to cut my mother out of my life.

On a random evening in October 2017, I was explaining my current relationship status with my mother to a close friend of mine. It was after a fight my mother and I had where she had ignored a clear boundary I had set between us. One she had previously agreed to. This woman can get me shrieking in a matter of seconds over the things she says and does. The result was me hanging up on her and texting her to inform her that "All contact is suspended until an appointment with a counsellor is set. These are my available dates." My friend's comment was something like: "It's odd/strange how much anger you have towards your mom. Like the same amount people have when they've been abused. But you can't seem to pinpoint anything she did to actually abuse you." This comment ate at me; because my friend was right. I was always angry at her, complaining about her, feeling like she was violating me or my life. We fought often, and I scrambled to repair often. I hated her. But I could never justify my hatred and anger; my dissension. I was confused and ashamed. I was flabbergasted with myself.

Until I called my best girl friend of 14 years to discuss the comment and how much it bothered me. Her words still ring like crystal: "Have you ever heard of gaslighting?" I put her on speaker phone and googled it at the same time she was explaining it. The universe got very small very fast. I think my response was "holy shit, my mom has been doing exactly that - all my life."

She admitted to me she had discovered her mom does that as well to a certain degree. I remember her telling me that after her own daughter was born, her mother had become more over imposing, controlling and critical than she could previously tolerate. My friend said it got so threatening that she finally told her mother to back off, or she wouldn't be allowed access to her granddaughter any more. She said her mother weighed her options and backed off - but still has a lot of emotionally abusive behavior. My friend just knows her mother's Achilles heel now.

I never knew this about my best friend. This was all news to me. Her and I got a much deeper understanding of why we were so similar and why our friendship has stood the test of time and distance. I'll take a moment to say "thank you" to her right here. I literally would not be on a path to healing right now without her immense courage to share her own struggle with me.

Fast forward to a little over a year later: November 2018. I actually can't remember the last time I spoke with my mother, answered or even opened an email or text from her. I actually sometimes forget she exists. It's so liberating.

Now when another family member tells me of an experience they have with her I can just laugh. We can just joke about her style of crazy. I can also shut down conversations about her and follow through on letting emotions about her go. I can 'choose' not to think about her. I can 'choose' to not get mad, or worked up. I can make her bullshit 'not my problem.'

I also now own my internal voice - which is the tool offered in Chapter 6. Her voice and commentary are no longer in my head. I can talk to myself in the way I would like to be spoken to. I can control internal criticism, I can offer myself support and I can trust my own beliefs and perceptions about the world around me. Most days. Which is an extremely reasonable level of accomplishment.

I can identify, accept and participate in healthy relationships. I can also identify and choose to not have relationships with people who don't respect my boundaries. I no longer feel obligated to participate in suggested plans from other people from fear of....so many weird/stupid things.

I also know how to repair. This was a huge triumph. I can have a disagreement with someone I love or care about and then can give, receive and even request an apology. Getting openly mad at someone doesn't mean the end of my relationship with them. Having someone get angry with me doesn't mean I am required to grovel and bend to their will to keep a relationship with them.

Best of all - I'm not so angry anymore. I spent a lot of my life angry. Angry at people. Angry about my life. Angry at my mother. Angry at myself. I had such a constant undertone of feeling wronged, a sense of indignation. I had no source for this. Through the exploration of a tool I discuss in Chapter 11, I was able to find where this came from. My constant rage and inability over the years to not identify the source or 'solve my problem' was exhausting. Constantly. I grew up thinking something was 'wrong with me.' Being able to identify where this came from and lift that lie off my shoulders changed my life drastically. Everything from diminishing daily fatigue, social discomfort, reactive behavior and especially for recognizing and owning my self worth.

December 2018

I attended a family event that my mother was present at. It was the first time I had come into contact with her in 14 months. Nothing exploded. Not me, not the event, nothing. I not only survived, but I walked away unharmed. Not a scratch on me. After over a year of cutting her out of my life and getting out of her choke hold.

Leading up to the gathering I was able to control my normal tendencies of running through 1 million scenarios where I imagine all of the hurtful or uncomfortable things she could say and do. And what I would do in return. I even had phone calls with relatives where they would bring up their own worry and concerns on my behalf:

> *What if she...*
> *What about (my daughter)....*
> *What are you going to do if...*
> *Are you going to be ok if...*

"My mum is going to do - what my mum's going to do. I can't control that. There's nothing I can do about that." I would respond. Her behavior was now none of my business and not my problem. Of course there were moments when anxiety would start - but the power I had now could control it. I could stop. I had mantras. I had tools.

I also - had better shit to do.

Such as: live my own life.

The life that was right in front of me. Not some 3 hour chunk of time, a week ahead of me. A chunk of time that I also had a huge amount of control over.

I arrived at my Aunt's house before my mum. I was greeted by warm, loving family. We caught up, talked about our lives, enjoyed all of the new children in our growing family. We connected. Then my mum showed up.

She looked a little surprised to see me.
She said hello.
She asked how I was.
I said hi back.
Told her I was good.
I asked how she was.
She said fine.
Then...we carried on.

I passively avoided and ignored her for the most part. It was wonderful. She moved around, talking to other family members, busied herself in the kitchen and helping her sister host, I guess. She also played with my daughter for a while.

A while later she asked my permission to offer things for my daughter's Christmas stocking. I could have interpreted this in SO many ways. I could see she was (either pretending or not) walking on eggshells with her approach to the topic. Possibly attempting to create a purposely uncomfortable social dynamic. I agreed - but also took the opportunity to communicate control:

"You may offer some." I put an ominous tone on 'some' and ended it with a dominant glare. We both knew it was in regards to my boundary about her bringing extra objects into my house without my permission.

She left shortly after this. I learned she was only on her lunch break from work. It was glorious. I had it in the back of my mind that I could leave early if I had enough of her. I had a whole exit strategy worked out. But didn't need it. One of my aunts made sure to catch me in the end though.

"What are your plans for Christmas? Are you seeing your parents?"

"I haven't made any plans to see them. I would be happy to see my dad but I have no intention of making plans with my mum."

tisk "That's still going on?" She clicked her teeth and made 'concerning eyebrows' at me.

I stared at her for a second. She was goading me. I just shrugged at her, gave a half smile and created body language to show the conversation was over. Then I occupied myself with one of the lovely new babies distributed around the room among my cousins. Not my monkey. Not my circus.

Upon leaving, I learned my mother had given my daughter a gift without telling me. It was a story book. When I read it to her on the way home, I had a momentary lapse where I wanted to burn the book. The story triggered all sorts of alarm bells and gaslighting, emotional abuse tactics. Even when I explained the story to my therapist at our next session - he was shocked at the rather obvious message.

"Wont you get lonely out there all by yourself?
Sometimes we have to be lonely to explore new things.
Will you come back to me one day?
Yes daddy, One day I'll come back to you"

But it took less than a few hours for me to let it go. The book was for my daughter. She was a complete innocent in the crossfire. My mum 'could' have given that book to my daughter with some sick, twisted, layered plan behind it. Or maybe - she didn't. I'll never know the truth. And there is no way to discover that truth.

This was the power I had now. I could just stop. I reacted at first with suspicion and some rage. But I could control it. I could curb it. I could forget about it. Her actions - her behavior - her intentions. I can choose how long it affects me for. I can exhale that bullshit and walk on.

Even the following few days when I got phone calls from family members to check in - there was nothing to say. There was nothing to talk about in regards to my mother. I left everything that had to do with crossing my mother's path - in the moment it happened.

Then I carried on with my life.

Now that I have let so much of it go, I can understand how confusing it is for others to imagine. Emotional abuse from a parent, their control and effect on us is so real. It's so strong. It is actually - crazy making. Though for someone not under that control and abuse… it simply seems prosperous. Some of my past recollections now perplex me, as to how I felt so out of control.

March 2019

I'm nearly finished this book and…I actually have a difficult time getting back into the headspace to finish parts of it. The memories and feelings are not as intense as they used to be. I can look back and remember that I used to fear what I would do if she showed up and knocked on my door. I would get myself into an anxious frenzy - walking through the steps of calling the police and trying not to physically assault her. I used to imagine pushing her down a set of stairs for looking at me from across the room with some shaming facial expression. I use to have nightmares about her coming up behind me at my car in a parking lot. What would I do?! How did she find me?! How will I get away from her?! My memories of the things she said and did to me as a teenager, young woman and new mother used to drain and exhaust me for days.

Emotional abuse victims are just a Human Volcano. Most of the time the molten lava churns below the surface, still dangerous but only internally destructive. Other times it erupts and destroys every living thing that's been unfortunate enough to put roots down nearby.

Now - I shrug at the thought or mention of her.

But what is more shocking is how the rest of my life has changed. The tools I applied and use to recover from that toxic upbringing have spread across my entire life. I feel like I've cured my own cancer. I didn't just remove my mother from my life. I got past the damage. I changed how I see myself and participate in everything.

I have found self confidence. I have found self worth. I have found self care. I have found a huge world of healthy friendships and connections. I have found and become the woman I want to be. I can also see the great woman I was yesterday and the better woman I can work at being tomorrow.

But I'm often just happy with the woman I am today. Not always. But often. Which is a substantial accomplishment.

Chapter 4
My Aggressive Philosophies

You have to **need** this. Badly.

When people leave abusive relationships or circumstances it is often at a point where anything is better than what they are experiencing. An event or realization hits them that offers a view into a world beyond where they are.

At 3 months old, my daughter was sleeping in one of those motorized swinging seats in front of our living room window. I was an extremely happy new mother. I had a healthy, happy pregnancy and birth. My partner and I were living outside of a small town surrounded by trees and nature in a big, 4 bedroom house. Deer came to visit our yard and our 3 cats roamed their vast grassland kingdom. The area was quiet, the air was fresh and the rent was cheap.

But at that moment - I was shrieking at my mother over the phone. Literally yelling, while my daughter slept, rocking back and forth in her tranquil little world of innocence. I was kneeling right in front of her just watching the swing go left to right. I was staring at her. The little love of my life. But yelling at my mother. Completely enraged.

It was that moment I had the thought **"I can't do this anymore."**

I had become aware of the energy I was bringing into my house, into my life, and around my daughter. It was negative, hateful, furious energy. It was as if I had experienced just a momentary wrinkle in time that made me realize: I never want to do this with my own daughter. I CAN'T have <u>this</u> in my life, at the same time as my daughter. The moment was intense for me.

Since the birth of my daughter, my mom had become more critical, insulting, manipulative, demanding and controlling than I could handle. It wasn't just 'my daughter.' It was more specifically 'her first grandchild.' She was now the holiest of Crones who would not be argued with on the subject of raising a child. Our arguments had become more explosive and dramatic right around the time I informed her I would be making my own family.

I discussed the epiphany with my partner afterwards. His comment was "I've been with you almost every day for 7 years and I have never seen you get as mad or react as badly to anyone, as you do with your mother."

Beyond Damage - Julia Gillis - 2019

It had to end. I needed a solution.

I'm not one to dilly dally. I'm an intense person. I'm aggressive. I really don't like doing anything half-assed. I love doing things the smartest way possible. The most effective. And I'm not afraid to tap my resources for this.

The smartest, most effective person I know - Is my brother. Warren Buffett has this guy that works closely with him, Charles Munger. It's said that this guy takes only seconds to get from A to Z in one move. My brother is just like that. I love it. Whenever I need advice - that's who I call. My own personal Charles Munger.

I called and explained what had been going on between mum and I. My brother was able to identify a cycle: I call her, I over share, she finds vulnerabilities, she preys on them, I get defensive, I lash out, she shames me, I apologize. We start over.

He says: break the cycle. One move. A to Z. Boom.

I was advised to stop sharing vulnerabilities with our mum.
I was advised to stop seeking help and advice from her.
I was advised to build a community of healthy female and matriarch style relationships with other women to replace the unhealthy one I was participating in with her.

This was the introduction of 'tea party talk' with my mum. I learned to keep topics about me short and sweet and to focus on talking about her and what she's up to.

This worked for months! It was amazing. Until she turned it into the problem.

Not having problems to share with her got twisted into "you're hiding things from me." Uuuuuggggggghhhhhhh.

More fights ensued. Shit got worse. Mother-daughter counselling happened. Shit got even worse. Then I cut her out. Then I discovered what gaslighting was. Then I hit rock bottom.

This. Was. Bullshit.

When I get depressed, I'm not often mopy. I'm more often disgruntled, pissy, grumpy, agitated, defensively sensitive, indignant, antisocial, masochistic and rudely apathetic.

Hitting rock bottom was the place I got to when I figured out I had been experiencing emotional abuse in my relationship with my mum. Which classified me as an emotional abuse victim. Which is shocking for anyone to 'discover' about themselves.

Some people like to ride that train; that 'woe is me' stuff.

I do not.

I do not like appearing weak, incompetent, fragile, helpless, pathetic, preyed on, easily influenced, soft, or any other word you can think of that goes with those ones.
It's not ok with me.

Being a *victim* - is **not** ok with me.

I needed to understand. I needed answers. I needed solutions. I needed tools. So I went hunting.

Being depressed, or even just feeling shitty about myself has never stopped me from doing 'something.' Even if I won't socialize or don't want to go to work, I still wind up doing something to occupy my time. I'll go through old things to throw out and clear clutter. I'll paint, draw, sketch, scrapbook or write. I'll knit a sweater while watching tragic British love stories. I'll make jewelry. Most of all, I'll read. I'll read everything I can get my hands on. So I read everything about gaslighting, emotional abuse, abusive parenting, narcissistic or emotionally unavailable mothers; all of it. In about 3 weeks.

I learned a lot. But I didn't get better. I actually got worse sometimes. It was torture. Why? Why am I not getting better? Do I want to stay like this? Am I going to be a damaged fuck up the rest of my life? Will I always sabotage myself and my life? Am I doomed to live in this constant self-hate cycle? How do I stop?

I asked these questions out loud to a friend. I was desperate. I didn't WANT to be depressed anymore. I didn't WANT to struggle anymore. Then I got handed my first tool.

Stop learning about how you're damaged.
Learn about how you can be better.

Stop dragging your heels and dragging your ass. Get on it. Get after it. Figure it out. No more whining.

This book is not for women who want to 'work it out' with their moms.
This book is for women who want to work themselves out.

This isn't a 'hippy dippy, take it easy, go slow' thing. This is fierce. This book is the life hack version for women raised by emotionally abusive mothers.

If this book is for you, it means you have lived your current lifetime under your mother's emotionally abusive control. That is disgusting. That is unacceptable. If you're mad - you should be. And you should be using that rage to fuel your desire to get better, have better and be better.

Be passionate about not carrying on a damaged legacy of love to the other people around you. It takes learning, it takes practice. The tools in this book are the ones children should be offered by loving caregivers. You were not. But it's never too late to change and never too late to learn.

If you were a victim and now you're a survivor, take the next step. Leave 'surviving' behind you and start 'thriving.' Become more than an accumulation of your past. <u>Be more than the sum of your parts.</u> You can live beyond what you know about your present or current self.

There is life beyond your damage. A life beyond your mother. A life that you control and have ownership of. A life that you can lay down in front of yourself, brick by brick, the way you want it to be. Lay that next brick and take that next step. Don't survive this life. Thrive in this life.

REWIRE YOUR BRAIN
Recap: Get aggressive about being a better person. Want this badly. Use whatever mental models or methods you need to psych yourself up for this. You need to become passionate about not repeating or carrying on the intergenerational legacy of abuse, pain & trauma in your family. You should see that as unacceptable behavior for someone as impressive as yourself. The time: is right now.

Here are some habits your need to start changing immediately. Not tomorrow or next week. Not 'when you are ready.' That's bullshit. You're just being lazy.

1) Collect your tools to get cut-throat with your mother (by reading this book.) Learn about boundaries, decide who you want to be; and decide who you DON'T want to be. Do not allow your mother to decide these things for you anymore. Do not even allow her to 'suggest' or 'insinuate' who you should be. <u>Your relationship with her is the ground zero war zone for learning how to thrive.</u>
2) When something in your life is bothering you, commit to changing it. Don't just whine and flail your hands about. Identify the true problem, decide what the best solution would be and make a plan. Then execute that plan. No excuses.

3) When people make suggestions about how you can fix problems going on in your life, stop - and think about what they've said. Ask yourself if the advice their offering is either constructive and helpful, or wishy-washy, self serving noise. If it's helpful, take it into consideration and add it to your tool bag of ways to rectify the problem. If it's not helpful, make a mental note to stop going to that person with your issues. You are wasting your time and energy trying to get help from that person. This includes your mother.

4) Decide who you want to be, and identify a path to becoming that person. Do you want to be someone who has self worth? Do you want to be someone who doesn't feel emotionally fragile around their mother? Do you want to be someone who feels they are successful? Do you want to be someone who doesn't mope around for a week after a normal human faux pas? Know who you want to be. Find your tools. Apply your tools. Change who you are. It's difficult - but it's not impossible. Which means its possible.

5) Cut out the people, behavior, habits, situations and activities that are not helping you. Get a 'big picture' view of your life and just start trimming the fat. Get rid of the excess. Become an emotional minimalist. Identify your essence and only do things that feed into who you want to be. Focus on the parts of your life that add VALUE while getting nit-picky about all the things that irritate you. Cut that shit out.

6) Believe that you are competent and capable of anything you set your mind too. Even if it doesn't look or turn out exactly how you imagined it in the beginning. Manifest your energy. Be passionate and be aggressive. Don't just want a better life; need it.

Chapter 5

Absorb Growth Style Knowledge

One of the most significant things I experienced during my healing process was the mindset change I had between absorbing information on 'who I am' vs. 'who I want to be.'

The reason I have such a harsh perspective towards the books that inform and educate on the topic of daughters with unloving mothers is their general effect on a person experiencing them. If you know anything about the power of the mind, you're aware of the many rules, quotes, statements and studies that support the following concept:

Each person is influenced by:
Their genetics
Their experiences
Their environment

These last 2 are what apply to my point. It's another version of 'you are what you eat.' Also: the **energy, things, & people** you surround yourself with will 'shape you.'

If you are constantly researching on how & why you are damaged

- this is all you will think about.

Let that shit go.

Move. On.

You will not find solutions there.

If you were raised with the same type of mum I had, you may also have the obsessive habit of collecting information, facts and understanding on any topic you come across. You leave no stone unturned, no source untapped, no book unread. That would be unacceptable. If it's important, you must become the expert - as to never appear unintelligent, unprepared, confused, or uncertain. This is vulnerability and it cannot be found within you. It will be preyed upon and used against you. I learned this from my mother (and her sisters & their own mother,) both directly and indirectly.

So of course I read multiple books on unloving mothers. And dragged my ass through a depression. For weeks. Continuing to read these books, looking for help. Looking for answers on 'why' I was who I was and to heal myself, fix myself; save myself.

Until that same friend whom made the prophetic comment about how I seem to dislike my mother for some undeterminable reason, at some point said to me "I think those books are holding you in a negative place."

Once again - mind blown.

And I put it to the test. Immediately. I jumped on the self-help, power of choice, 'you're awesome!' literary bandwagon.

2 audio books later I commited to 3 goals:
1) Start modeling again (I was 28 and hadn't done this since I was 21)
2) Start martial arts (and work towards learning Krav Maga)
3) Get a motorcycle license (I've wanted this since I was 13)

I crushed all 3 goals in a month. Literally a month. It was exactly within 30 days that I had my first photoshoot, signed up for and started Taekwondo and completed not just my written motorcycle test, but completed a full course and first level drivers' test. These are goals I had been sitting on for over 15 years. All suppressed by a continued obsession and participation in my toxic upbringing.

The power of these books is 2 fold. First, they offer actual tools, concepts and ideas that you can apply through action in your life. The second (this is a big one): they are supportive. They believe in you. They state over and over again: you can do this! These books become both your cheerleader and your loving Nanny. They feed your endless emotional starvation with a true substance: healthy support mixed with positive guidance.

Women who have been raised with poorly bonded mothering did not receive either of those things. They often describe a feeling of a hole somewhere within them. The feeling is manifested so deeply or strongly that it is often described as a physical feeling. A place within us that is missing; a hole or void. It is our internal damage that we try desperately to hide from others. We try to ignore, cover up or fill this 'empty/hollow' space with many things: control issues, eating issues, over achievement, drug and alcohol abuse, self sabotage, hardlined privacy, dangerous sexual behavior, over dependant relationship styles, obsessive-compulsive habits; the list goes on.

What I believe to be 'missing' is that healthy bond which is supposed to be created by our main caregiver. Victims of more apparent childhood abuse have this same experience too. A feeling of not being complete and they display many of the same behaviors. It comes from having a caregiver who doesn't know how to offer love within the boundaries of healthy bonding, support and guidance.

The positive 'self-help' or personal development literature is an extremely safe and nonthreatening way to start receiving this type of healthy, supportive guidance that we missed out on as children. In the beginning, it is so important to find a venue to receive support without feeling vulnerable. The books, blogs, videos & podcast are just media. They can't judge you or prey on you. The books don't criticize you. They aren't designed and worded to make you feel like an incompetant or inadequate person. They allow you multiple opportunities to interpret their meaning and find extra layers that are even more positive and helpful as you revisit them; time and time again.

This source of support and guidance isn't limited to books either. I consumed a lot of this 'support & guidance' from audiobooks while driving to and from work. You can also find self development podcasts, Youtube videos, even just random blogs about setting healthy boundaries and engaging in positive self growth behavior or goal setting.

Choosing literature (or videos, podcasts, etc) which repeatedly offers you options and tools on how to become the person you want to be <u>changes your thought patterns.</u>

Absorbing knowledge about 'who you are right now' or 'who you used to be' <u>holds you in that place.</u>

Stop surrounding yourself with information about the past and present 'you'. Start surrounding and immersing yourself in information, energy, support and guidance that offers ways for you to become the person you hope to be.

What is extremely important about this tool is to replace the beliefs your shitty, toxic, emotionally abusive mother gave you about yourself and the world. This is key. **You are rewiring your brain to identify, accept and crave positive, healthy support.**

Material that helped me:

You are a Badass - Jen Sincero

(I cannot emphasize how much this book has helped me. I listen to it in audiobook form every few months. It's probably unhealthy codependency - I don't give a shit. This book is now my mother.)

The Subtle Art of Not Giving A Fuck - Mark Manson (amazing on audio book)
Super You - Emily V. Gordon
Unf*ck Your Brain - Podcast by Kara Loewentheil (This is another pseudo mother that I have inducted into my tribe)
Learned Optimism - Daniel E. P. Seligman (I was gifted this book by my oldest brother while in early university. It was a game changer)
The 4 Hour Work Week - Tim Ferriss (All of Tim's work is useful or helpful. You're literally a big dumb dumb if you don't know who he is.)
The 4 Hour Body - Tim Ferriss
Happier Now - Nataly Kogan
Mind Gym - Gary Mack
Change Anything - Joseph Grenny, Kerry Patterson, Al Switzler, David Maxfield, Ron McMillan
TED Talks - all of them, any of them.

Next Level Books:

Breaking the Habit of Being Yourself - Joe Dispenza
(This book involves quantum physics. Don't pass it off as too complex. It's incredible & necessary. You are intelligent enough to absorb this.)

REWIRE YOUR BRAIN

Recap: Our environment and the way we experience it molds and shapes us significantly. Harness and utilize this knowledge to your benefit. Design your own environment to be full of information and experiences that allow you to expand into your ideal self. Have voices, literature, media that encourages a growth style mindset. Insight is great, but increase the amount of time you spend looking forward.

Tips on ways to do this:

Start at your library, amazon, spotify, youtube, anywhere, everywhere. Find books that have a voice your 'most optimistic self' can connect to or get on board with. The Jen Senchero book is honestly an all time favorite. She's not soft, doesn't speak to you like a child, and encourages you to call yourself on your own bullshit, while telling you that you're capable of incredible things. If you put in the effort.

Make it a hobby. Make it a challenge. Make it a game. Anything. Get obsessed with ways to start reading and listening to anything that is sending the message that you have the power to change, get better, be better and accomplish all of the things you've always wanted to. Find voices and words that are constantly telling you that you are capable, competent, and worthy. And believe them. Start getting used to positive self talk. It's not cheesy (or doesn't have to be.) You have time for this.

And most of all, have this material replace anything that is explaining what is 'wrong' with you. Throw that shit out the window, in the garbage and on the fire. That person is done. That time is over. You need to look at the 'broken you' in mirror and walk away from that person. That person is your past and you are moving forward. They have a place in the memories of how you used to think of yourself - but they are no longer determining who you are or who you're going to be.

Chapter 6
Take Ownership of Your Internal Voice

Internal Commentary

Psychological studies have determined that the 'voice inside our head' or the way we speak to ourselves is actually a strong derivative of our main caregiver's voice. For those of us with narcissistic mothers, it's their voice. Our subconscious is an adopted form of our main caregiver's speech patterns, worry, advice, reactions, perspectives. All of it.

Example:
Healthy Mothering: It's ok to make mistakes. Everything will be ok. We all fail sometimes. Don't worry, you can try again. I'm right here if you need help.

Unhealthy Mothering: What were you thinking? You should know better. I just don't understand. I raised you better than that. I'll have to call Ms. Smith and explain what happened. I wish you would have come to me first. Why would you do something like that?

Now think about the last time you did something wrong or disappointed yourself. How did you speak to yourself? Did the words you used to hear from your mother flood your head and slash you with red hot pokers? I bet. And it's fucking toxic.

This was one of the most effective exercises my therapist and I discovered together. I needed to change the way I spoke to myself. Everyone has hundreds of conversations with themselves, every day. We are constantly commenting on our own behavior and choices. We chastise and scold, we comfort and encourage, we question and assess. We do this in almost the exact same way we were spoken to as children growing up. Just like the example above - there are healthy ways to do this....and unhealthy ways.

I had a lot of very unhealthy ways of talking to myself. I degraded, badgered and shamed myself. I was unsupportive and relentless. When I made a mistake, failed, had an embarrassing social moment - the commentary was horrible. I could never let it go or brush it off or allow myself forgiveness. When I accomplished something, it was never good enough, I down played my role or my efforts. If I was sick or depressed, I was even harder on myself for not being able to get through a normal day or keep up with my responsibilities. There was no self care, no self compassion. And if someone else hurt me or my feelings or crossed a boundary, it was my fault. I was just overreacting, being too sensitive or being weak.

I would never speak to someone else like this. Unless I hated them. Even a stranger. I would have to be horribly mad at anyone to talk to them that way. But I spoke

Beyond Damage - Julia Gillis - 2019

to myself this way. And I was spoken to this way. I was made to feel this way about myself through the example set by how I was spoken to growing up.

Most of all, I would NEVER speak to my own daughter this way. Which is where my therapist and I got the idea.

When I decided to become a parent, I was constantly researching and seeking the best ways to parent. If anyone tells you there's no manual for parenting - they're full of shit. There are hundreds. There are thousands. There are so many books, blogs, & articles about parenting, all with different tools, tips, perspectives and methods. If you're literate, you have access to decades of research and advice on how to be a great parent. There is literally no fucking excuse today.

When considering how I was going to raise my daughter I was very diligent about my choices and tried my best to 'be aware' and make conscious decisions about my actions and responses with her. When I would comfort or encourage or discipline my daughter I would think about how I would have wanted to be spoken to at that age. I find I am always 'the most kind' to my daughter. The most patient. The most compassionate. The most empathetic. The most encouraging. I feel that's the role of a mother. You're 'their person.' They test their boundaries the most with you, they are the most raw with you. They are the most free to discover the world and be themselves with you. As a child's mother, I believe it's my role to be the safest person for them to do all of those things with. We are the only people designed to love them unconditionally. And to rob a child of that person in their life is horrific and damaging. Obviously.

So my therapist and I decided that I should apply the same concepts to my self talk. When I'm tired, struggling, or frustrated I need to turn towards myself with compassion and ask questions first. Am I underslept or malnourished? Is something upsetting me or making me uncomfortable? Am I overstimulated or taking on too much? I need to find the source of my own negative experience or behavior and go through the list of healthy ways to address that. Then answer those needs with love and patience.

When I accomplish things or do a good job at something - I need to give myself credit. I need to congratulate and reward myself with positive reinforcement. I need to identify and label good habits so when I'm making mistakes I have a reservoir of language to turn the situation around.

We need to have this same level of reverence for the ripple effect our words have on ourselves, as they do on a child. We need to honor this by making conscious choices about how we talk to ourselves. Most importantly, if the voice we are currently using is broken or causing harm - we need to make changes.

External Commentary

How we hear our main caregiver(s) talk to us creates our self talk. In addition to this, how we hear them talk about the rest of the world shapes our thought patterns regarding the external world. In some instances, during childhood or adolescence we see things in our parents that we hate. We then vow to 'never' do that, or be the opposite. But there is often a level of unconscious dialogue that we pick up. We then use this to describe the world around ourselves.

Growing up, I watched my parents remain at the dinner table after the meal was finished almost every night. They would spend upwards of an hour talking about their day. They would share stories about their bosses' and coworkers' incompetence. They would talk about how mismanaged their place of work was and how it 'should' be organized. They shared all of the injustices and negative things going on and happening to them or around them. The narrative of what was happening at their jobs was constantly some astonishing tragedy of other peoples' stupidity or lack of emotional intelligence.

When I would go out places with my mum, she would talk out loud about her dissatisfaction with everything. "Who would organize it this way? Well that's not a very smart design. You know, if they would just figure out how to… I don't understand why someone would… People need to learn how to…" It was endless. Nothing anyone was doing was proper, correct, or as well done as she could do it. No one understood as well as she did, about anything. Her commentary about the world was critical; and with the status of a saint. She was 'just trying to help people.' Even if they didn't want it or didn't need it. Throughout my childhood, I watched her approach complete strangers in public, offering to help them or offering uninvited comments on what they were doing. Often she was directive or instructional, becoming the manager of whatever activity she was interrupting.

There was also something just a little bit wrong with the way her hairstylist did her hair. Or how a dentist cleaned her teeth. Or how the person took and executed her coffee order. Or how a playground was designed. Nothing was as it should be. Nothing was ever good enough.

In my early 20s I had started spending enough time away from her and with other people, that I built an awareness of having dark shades of this behavior within myself. I could actually be quite ruthless in my criticism of others; and the world in general. I felt I had the responsibility of informing people of their incompetence and pointing out the follies of any system I didn't find adequately organized. I eventually gained enough perspective to see how unpleasant, confrontational, and shitty this was. (By 'gain perspective' I mean that people dished it back, put me in my place and offered some choice words on how to stop being a complete asshole; and I listened to them. Sometimes.) It wasn't just unwelcome in friendships, partnerships and work environments - it was personally and internally exhausting. It was a constant tone of dissatisfaction with the world.

This is actually a really basic concept. It's how racist parents raise racist kids. How religious parents raise religious kids. It's how West Coast hippy parents raise West Coast hippy kids. It's also how positive, driven, disciplined, open minded, brilliant people raise positive, driven, disciplined, open minded kids.

In a more relatable fashion, it's how toxic mothers raise toxic daughters. As we listen to our mothers communicate their perspective of the world around them, we build that dialogue in our own world too.

REWIRE YOUR BRAIN
Recap: We need to get rid of the default voice. It's not helping us and it never worked properly in the first place. That entire software system needs to be replaced. The conversations you are having with yourself, about yourself and about other people are not healthy. It is time to design your own.

Rewire Internal Commentary
Every time you start talking to yourself in a negative way or talking to yourself the way your mother did - stop. Recognize how you are currently talking to yourself. Gain awareness of the moments you start shaming, chastising or punishing yourself.

Then - Switch: to the language, tone and phrases you wished you heard from your mother. Or how you speak to the people in your life you love the most. Change your words to the understanding, empathetic, supportive words you would use with any child or person you love. You won't catch yourself every time - at the beginning. It takes practice. Some days will be harder than others. But if you keep trying and keep reminding yourself - you can accomplish changing your inner voice to one that you own and control. It will change your life.

Completely replace the following phrases:
I always
I never
I should/shouldn't

Also remember fluid acceptance. After you feel you've changed how you speak to yourself, you might have a really hard day, or be faced with a really devastating challenge and revert back to the old voice. That's ok. The first step is recognising it - and to tell yourself it's ok to fall. It's ok to make mistakes. It's ok to not be great all the time. That's too much to expect of anyone. We are all in the same boat. We all struggle sometimes. That's ok. Find help. Pick yourself back up after taking a break. Get back out there. It's going to be ok. It will be more than ok.

Keep working at it. Don't give up on changing this. Listen to how you support your friends and loved ones. Use those words and phrases on yourself. You are worthy of your own love, kindness and empathy.

Even if you start talking to yourself in a negative way, you can back up. You can
1. Stop
2. Forgive
3. Back up
4. Start again
5. Begin differently

(The book *Learned Optimism* really helped me with this change.)

Another option is to go find someone you know who already has the language you want to adopt or start using. Tell them directly what you need. Tell that person you need hear someone offer positive reinforcement. This is not a crazy request. Especially to someone who already speaks that way to people. They already know how great it feels, that's why they do it. Repeat their words, out loud to yourself. Either in front of them, or after meeting with them. It's about practice and building a habit. Then turning that habit into behavior, then elevating that behavior into a personality trait.

My success story from this exercise:
In May of 2018 I had an under the muscle breast augmentation. I'm a major gym rat and before the surgery had been working on being able to do regular, full plank dude-style push ups. I was really happy with what I had accomplished, but knew with surgery coming up, I would have to start all over again. I did all the research to learn how and when to safely get back to the gym and work upper body after breast implants. It was around the same time my therapist and I had implemented 'changing my inner voice.' After a few months back at the gym I was doing elevated pushups on a smith machine. Each week lowering the bar closer to the ground and getting more body weight on my pectorals.

At first I was just proud of getting back to the gym and was riding that high. After a few weeks I was getting a bit hard on myself, specifically about my pushup progress. "Why aren't you further ahead? What are you doing wrong? Shouldn't you be able to do more than this? You're supposedly in better shape than most women. Why can't you do X yet? You need to get after it harder." A few weeks later, after still progressing at the gym and working on my inner voice I had a shocking moment while doing push ups. I was telling myself "Keep going, almost there, you can do it. Don't give up. One more! You got this!" I came out of my set like "What was I just saying?!"

I had that moment. Not just "omg, I did all those push-ups." It was "omg, I talked to myself so nicely! I was so awesome to myself!" I actually texted a friend immediately to tell them. I was so proud of myself! It was pretty great. That was a public happy dance moment.

Rewire External Commentary

1. Take all the moments you create external dialogue and break them down into sections. Most important are the types of people you actually come into contact with or share space with.
    a. Strangers you see doing things in public.
    b. Other moms, parents, women you know socially.
    c. Your employers & work colleagues.
    d. Family members/relatives.

When you start to have thoughts, comments or opinions about them, recognize what those sounds like. Are you judging? Are you criticizing? Are you blaming? Do you sound like your mother?

2. Take a moment to remember why your mother thinks about the world outside herself in such a negative way. People are abusive to others as a (toxic and horrible) defense mechanism. Their best defense is an offence. They pick on, degrade, and hurt others in order to protect their scared, vulnerable, small, insecure selves. They are attacking everything they don't understand. Especially when someone is a narcissist - they have no empathy. They can't imagine 'why' someone else is doing something. They are unable to put themselves in someone else's shoes.

You are not a narcissist. You are capable of empathy. Which means when a stranger, or person you know socially, or work colleague or family member/partner is doing something you either don't understand or think is stupid - you can put yourself in their shoes. Even just for a second. Then remember that no matter who you are and what you're doing - tolerance, understanding and compassion are the best route. For everything. If you are being observed in any capacity, doing anything publicly - what thoughts or feelings would you want people to have about you as they watch you? Remember the way your mother talks about the world and other people: would you wish that upon anyone else? No. Then why would you offer it too?

3. Take a second to humble yourself. Admit that you don't know. You don't know what is actually going on or why. You might not have a clue. About anything. You might not have any fucking idea why someone is acting a certain way or doing a certain thing. Furthermore - it might be none of your goddamn business.

Learning humility will put a very healthy amount of distance between who you are and the person your mother seems to be.

4. Change your tone. The tone of your commentary about your eternal surroundings is directly correlated to your attitude. Especially if it's similar to your mother's. We all know the tone. It's the rhetorical, bitchy, arrogant tone. The tone you take when you've already decided you're right. You've already decided that whatever and whoever your commenting on is an idiot.

   Replace it with a new tone. My favorite is 'curious.' This is my favorite because it allows a transition from total bitch to politely sarcastic or facetious to compassionately inquisitive.

Example:
- Bitchy Rhetorical tone: WHY would someone do that?!
- Sarcastic tone: Whhhyyyyy.......would someone do that......
- Compassionately Inquisitive tone: I wonder why someone would do that?

Your attitude of being annoyed and commenting rhetorically needs to change to a place of curious empathy.

5. Use "I wonder..."
   - If that person needs help
   - If that person is having a difficult day
   - If I can't see everything going on
   - If maybe someone tried that already and it didn't work
   - If that's really any of my business
   - If I'm actually the one causing the issue
   - If I could look at this in a different way
   - What questions I could ask to understand this better

You're not perfect. No one else is perfect. No system is designed perfect. Every person, situation, and system exists in a gradient. Every person has great days and total disaster days. Every situation unfolds differently depending on the people and circumstances that are present. Every system functions more or less adequately depending on the needs of each unique person utilizing it.

Next Level:

Whether you want to master this or find yourself struggling with these concepts, a great place to continue exploring is Buddhism. This Eastern philosophy has endless material to help a person develop and practice ideas such a compassionate witnessing, living passively, acceptance on a cosmic scale and loving kindness.

There are thousands of gurus, paths of teaching and different ways to have these concepts explained. If it interests you at all - absorb this growth style knowledge. And don't be discouraged by certain meditation styles or explanations. Keep reading, keep exploring, keep asking questions - something or someone will resonate and help.

Chapter 7
Stop Blaming

If you're going to get better, you need to stop looking back and start looking forward. You also need to stop WASTING ENERGY. This is the moment; right now, as you read this - to decide to stop blaming your mother for who you are.

If you haven't come across the differences between fault and responsibility - this section is very important. If you have come across these explanations before - this should reinforce it.

Who you have become <u>might be</u> your mother's fault.

Who you want to be is <u>absolutely</u> your responsibility.

<u>Know The Difference</u>

Blame is about fault.
Responsibility is about accountability.

Blame & fault are most often about past events.
Responsibility & accountability are most often about present events.

If you don't like who you are and how your life is going - it is up to you to make the changes you want to see. Look in front of you. Look ahead of you. You control that playing field and where you put your energy.

The abuse and trauma dished out by your mother is her fault. The survival tactics you developed are her fault. The wounds and scars you have from her are her fault. Her not knowing how to love you… is not her fault. But it is her responsibility. One that she has clearly struggled with and is not solving. Which is not your responsibility. But what you're going to DO about that - is.

Your awareness of this offers you the opportunity of choice, control and change. Take it. Stop participating in actions and behaviors that aren't effective and aren't helping you. Here is a list of some of those things:

● Waiting for or demanding an apology from your mother
● Waiting for or organizing reconciliation with your mother

- Negotiating your boundaries with your mother
- Feeling guilt and shame about who you are
- Being angry with your mother about things she has done
- Being angry with your mother about things she is currently doing
- Digging up and reliving painful memories of how your mother raised you or treated you
- Thinking of yourself as an abuse victim
- Thinking of yourself as damaged
- Thinking that any part of who you are is permanent
- Blaming your mother for who you are

Even: blaming yourself for who you are.

None of these activities are helpful or productive.

It's not just about blame, but it's one of the most common ways of wasting energy for people who have suffered past abuse. It is time to stop participating in all things that use up your precious energy in unproductive ways. Every emotion we experience is using energy, just like every activity we do: going for a run, working out a budget, planning a birthday party - all of these things require energy. So does joy, love, grief, jealousy, reflection and...?

You got it - blaming. Blaming anyone for anything.

Even if you would currently like to hold your mother responsible or accountable for how she is treating you now, there is nothing further you can do after that. That is a dead end activity. It is her choice to take on blame, fault, responsibility or accountability. What she does with that is not something you can control. You can't force her behavior or response. Also - your mother taking blame or fault, will not change what happened. But you are still responsible and accountable to yourself in regards to how those situations affect you, right now. You only have control of yourself, in the present.

This is all about where you're going to put your energy from now on. Every person only has so much time; in a day, in a week, in a lifetime. You need to devote the energy you have access to towards things that will make an impact on your life in a positive direction. If you spend your 16 waking hours thinking about your mother and how much she bothers you and how aggravating it is that she doesn't own up to doing hurtful things to you, that is 16 hours of energy you didn't spend honoring yourself. It's 16 hours you didn't focus on bossing your career, or loving your children, or establishing whether or not the new guy you're dating is displaying red flags. Even if you're splitting your energy doing those things at the same time while being resentful about your relationship with your mother - you are half-assing things you could be crushing at 100%.

There are 3 different stories I want to share that helped me form perspective on letting go and having awareness on where I put my energy.

My Charles Munger – Round 2

"Can I offer you some advice?"

"Andrew, if you ever have advice for me, I want it. You never have to tiptoe into that. You give the best advice out of anyone I've ever known. If you've got some, I want it."

"Stop talking about her."

This was my brother, again. Boom. One move. Obviously more of a conversation ensued after his advice, but the point was clear from the get go.

I had spent the previous evening at his place with him, his wife, and one of my aunts. The ladies present (myself included) were all talking about my mom, while my brother tidied up the kitchen in silence. Memories, issues, the mind boggling, crazy behavior; we spent a good part of 2 hours talking about her and topics involving her. Much like I had been doing for the past 8 - 10 months that I had cut her out. That was the crazy part. I had cut her out - but she was the majority of what I talked about or thought about. I was obsessed with my relationship with my mother. It took up almost all of the space in my life. I couldn't stop feeding the beast.

My brother pointed out the buffet I had laid out, to keep the beast alive. Every time I thought about her, talked about her, complained about her, got dragged into a story about her, I was keeping her in my life. This gave her 'control' of me. I was volunteering my energy to her. Even though I had cut her out of my life - I surrounded myself with her. It was sick.

Stop talking about her.

Put Her Down

Around this same time, my father told me a story from eastern philosophy about 2 monks. One monk was older and had been practicing for much longer while the other monk was younger and new to the teachings. They had left the monastery and were, I believe, delivering a message to another monastery quite a distance away.

They came to a river where the bridge had washed away. There was a woman standing at the edge, attempting to get across but the river was too strong or deep for her. But one of the practices the monks followed was to have no contact with women. The older monk decides to help her anyway and picks her up and carries her across the river. He puts her down on the other side and both parties carry on their paths.

A few kilometers down the road the young monk finally stops and says something like "I can't believe (or I don't understand why) you picked up that woman. We are not suppose to have contact with women. It's against the teaching!"

The older monk simply turns to the younger one and says "Yes, but I put her down 4 kilometers ago. Why are you still carrying her?"

You need to put your mom down. Stop carrying her.

Why it's (probably) Called Baggage

Ever notice that when you have to carry a bag of groceries for 2 or 3 blocks, it starts out easy then as your walk goes on, the bag feels heavier? You haven't added groceries, and the ones you're carrying haven't gotten heavier. It's your energy. You have been using it and exerting it. As time goes on, if you don't rest, or put those groceries down, your body gets worn down. You run out of energy. By the time you get home, you can barely get in the door let alone put the groceries in the cupboard. That's what people are talking about when they use the term 'baggage.' It's exhausting; and just gets heavier the longer you carry it. Continuing to carry it will rob you of the energy you require to keep living your life.

The longer you carry her. The more she will weigh. The more energy it will cost you.

All of these stories are perspectives on how we waste energy holding onto unnecessary things. Spending any energy on blame and fault towards your mother (or anyone else) does not produce any results. It's just you sending energy outwards; specifically negative energy. So if you are getting anything back from it; it's negative in return. Don't feed that cycle. Don't feed that beast. Don't carry that beast.

If or when you stop obsessing over your mother, you will find a shocking amount of spare time. Shocking. Can you list all the moments of your life you waste energy on your mother?
a)   Fighting with her
b)   Being anxious before having contact with her
c)   Being depressed or upset after you have contact with her
d)   Going over things that have happened between you while you're doing chores, driving to work, playing with your child, trying to fall asleep
e)   Furturizing situations that might come up between you while you're doing chores, driving to work, playing with your child, trying to fall asleep
f)   Talking to other people about her; things she's done, things she's doing, things you're worried she will do
g)   Considering how she will react to your personal decisions (changing your hair, moving homes, your choice in partner, how you arrange your living room furniture, etc.)

Beyond Damage - Julia Gillis - 2019

All of this... is bullshit. Especially because we know the cycle. It doesn't end at just going through the facts. We start analyzing and picking it apart. Trying to find rhyme and reason behind what did, what is or what will happen. We want to find a source. We want to blame someone when things make us angry, hurt us or threaten us.

Imagine the amount of energy used in the above examples. Give it an actual quantity. If the majority of your week is spent on these things, what would that look like?
- An hour before you see her/talk to her (once a week)
- An hour with her (once a week)
- An hour after you see her (once a week)
- The 20 minute drive to and from work every day = 40 minutes a day = 3.33 hours a week.
- Half the time you spend with your child every week?
- An hour a day of chores = 7 hours a week
- An hour every night trying to fall asleep = 7 hours a week
- 5-20 minutes every time you're about to make a choice that she'll see and comment on.

That's over 20 solid hours that you might be spending on negative energy involving your mum. Every week. Minimum.

If you stop: you will free up SO MUCH ENERGY. You will sleep better. You will live better. You will love and play and succeed better. Every day. Every moment you 'used to' spend on her - will be free. You will be free to day dream, plan, talk about positive things, be present. This change in energy will shock you. That beast you've been feeding, that person you've stopped carrying, that baggage you no longer drag around - will make you feel like you can sprint so hard, you'll launch yourself off this planet.

REWIRE YOUR BRAIN
Recap: All of the energy that you are using to blame your mother, talk about her, think about her, hold her accountable, be angry with her - is being wasted. If she is truly a narcissist, abusive, or unloving then none of the energy you put into her is going to have a positive outcome. You need to put all of your energy where it will count the most. You need to free up the energy you've been wasting and see how incredible your life can become when you put that energy in worthwhile places.
Tools, tips and habits to stop wasting time on blame:
1) Every time you have a thought about your mum in the past tense - stop. Then pick a mantra:
    a) That happened in the past. It won't change. How does that situation affect me right now and what can I do about that?

b) That was then and this is now. That situation is not currently happening. What is happening right now? Who am I with, what am I feeling, what am I about to be doing? What do I wish I was doing?

c) I can't change what she did, but I can change how I feel. I don't have to be angry. I can have empathy. I can release that resentment.

d) That situation made me angry/sad/hurt/etc. What can I do right now to release those feelings about the past?

2) Every time you have a thought about your mum in the future tense - stop. Then pick a mantra:
   a) I cannot see the future. There is no point imagining what she will do. I need to focus on what's in front of me.
   b) I have a life right in front of me that I need to live. I cannot control the future. I cannot control my mum. All I can control is myself.
   c) Furturizing is not a productive use of my time. It will not create the future I want to participate in.

3) Every time you find yourself talking about your mum - stop. Then pick a mantra:
   a) Talking about this isn't productive.
   b) Talking about this isn't a good use of my time.
   c) Talking about this won't change what has/will happen.

4) Notice how much less time you spend thinking about and talking about your mum when she is not around. Then redirect all of that energy into positive and productive places in your life.
   a) Get better sleep
   b) Focus on whatever your hands are doing and enjoy it
   c) Think about something you enjoy doing or people you enjoy being with
   d) Manifest your goals
   e) Manifest love for your life and yourself
   f) Laugh harder and louder
   g) Get the 'resting bitch' look off your face (for a few seconds)

5) Then start applying these tools to all the other times you find yourself placing blame or resentment on others. Road rage, having your boundaries crossed, a server at a restaurant, coworkers. You get the drill. Have self awareness - stop - pick a mantra - breath deep - adjust your attitude - move the fuck on.

Chapter 8

Better & Good vs. Competent & Capable

This tool was one of the most interesting to discover and exciting to repeat. It's also one of the more challenging to exercise regularly.

In the western world a trend has developed around 'Self-care.' Especially for women. The list of activities suggested as self care have a range from 'actually healthy' all the way to marketing tricks to provoke you into being a higher consumer. I absolutely support the idea of making time once a week to take a well deserved bath with a glass of wine and a book or every 4-6 months go on a nature retreat or take a meditation weekend. Of course it also feels good to say 'fuck it' and ignore the chores to curl up on the couch with ice cream and cheetos to binge watch that new Netflix show. Or have a crazy night out with the girls on the Visa. (Let's get the sugary drinks, and extra cheesy nachos then dance the night away like idiots!)

There are a huge number of other things in between that we use to make ourselves feel better or feel good when we are struggling with something. We go on juice diets, we do a spring cleaning of the house, we avoid facebook & social media for a month, or even join a club or group activity. These things are great and they are helpful for a lot of people who are having some very normal struggles.

We are urged (or we feel the need) to participate in these things to de-stress from being overworked, recover from a break up, gain back confidence in our body image, to feel we have a life outside of parenting/work or refresh a lost passion for life.

But constantly feeling like an inadequate human being because you were raised with low self worth is not a normal struggle. Being raised to believe that love needs to be 'earned' is not a normal struggle. This is where toxic and addictive behavior comes from in people; used as methods for self soothing and self preservation. These addictions can come in obvious forms: smoking, shopping, cleaning, drinking, perfectionism. They can also come in more hidden addictive behaviors: cutting off friends or partners after one disagreement, keeping your life so busy you never stop to have self reflection, having sleep problems, living a different 'role' or persona with certain people to never be known deeply, or avoiding participation in anything you are not certain you will do well at.

Both the 'self-care' methods as well as the obvious addictive behaviors are used to soothe all types of people in times of struggle. These are the things that make us feel better or good - for a short time. They can also be helpful in just pressing the reset button for people in a slump. But for adult children of unloving or emotionally abusive mothers this slump feels like a pit you are incapable of crawling out of. Literally incapable. It's this infinite loop of warped and useless efforts. No matter what you do or accomplish or try, you wind up in the same place: feeling like you don't know what you're doing, nothing is ever good enough and your life is an endless cycle of futile, half-rate accomplishments.

First things first: recognise that self-care activities (and addictive behaviors) are not what you need. They will not EVER fix what you are feeling. Not ever.

Second: replace the concept of doing things that make you feel 'good or better' with the concept of doing things that confirm you are a 'competent and capable' person. This is the tool that will actually start lifting the veil of false perspectives about you and about the world.

Owning Your SUCCESSES

One of the biggest reasons that people feel like failures is because they have allowed some exterior source to be their evaluator of success. That's a mistake any normal person can make. But daughters of emotionally abusive mothers get an extra treat. Just like we absorb our mother's voice as our own internal dialogue, we are conditioned to believe in her specific framework for what success looks like. An additional issue with this is her framework is designed to not be achievable. This is often the narcissism and gaslighting at play.

There are many family types that also follow the intergenerational behavior of deciding for their children what success looks like. The key difference is the parents have realistic and achievable standards for this. When parents really want their child to become a doctor, lawyer or banker that can be a lot of pressure. But when the child becomes one, the parents are proud and communicate that in a number of ways. That falls in a relatively healthy upbringing category.

But when raised with an unloving mother, nothing is ever good enough. You could run a community centre or a country and she would still point out your short comings. If you've done your research you already know this comes from a number of screwed up places. It could be anything from jealousy of watching her daughter be more successful than her or a sick desire to have you continue begging for her approval or the belief that complimenting you is bad parenting and will spoil you.

Your goals to use this tool are:
1) Identify or uncover the standards for success that came from your mother (one of the writing exercises in Chapter 11 will help you with this.)
2) Make a list of things you've always wanted to do

3) Decide on your own rubric of what would make you 'successful' in that regard
4) Start fucking doing them

Obviously number 4 is the hard part. But this is a great place to apply fluid acceptance. This is an incredible way to participate in the grey zone. This is because when you get to step 3, you get to decide what success looks like. You decide what your standards of failure or success are - and - you can change them whenever-the-fuck-you-want.

I can easily use an example:
1) I learned through my mother that modeling and acting are not appropriate, sustainable or suitable ways of making a living when you are an intelligent or capable woman.
2) Growing up I obsessively fantasized about being a model or actress. I never let that dream go and I constantly felt like I was not living up to the potential of a gift or talent I felt I possess by not following that passion
3) At the age of 28 I knew I wouldn't be walking the runways of Milan. But I made realistic goals for my age, physique and access to opportunity. If I could get paid for just 3 modeling shoots (whether it was $20 or $200, it didn't matter) and get called in for 3 casting calls - I would feel I had done 'something.' I could die without regret.
4) I made a plan. Start working with pro bono photographers. This would help me get a portfolio started. Then sign up for a course that helps people create a comp card for casting calls and how to present yourself in those auditions. Then - who knows? Just get going.

I did the same with martial arts. I did the same with my motorcycle license. I did the same with writing this book.

Just get started. It's all the small wins. This is how you will rewire your brain.

My martial arts goal is to be competent in Krav Maga. Before I started, I was scared. Scared of group classes, scared of not knowing what I was doing, scared of being the beginner, scared to fail, scared of judgement, scared of disappointing myself and an instructor. So I designed a system of easy progression for myself. I signed up for a 3 class trial of Taekwondo. I showed up and accepted the support from people ahead of me. I got comfortable being the beginner. I learned that other people are, more often than not, supportive, positive and encouraging when you're new at something. Then I signed up for 3 trial classes of kickboxing. After that I will either continue with kickboxing until I want to move on or I will find a Krav Maga trainer. I started in a place where 'failing' was so hard. All I had to do was show up to class. I wasn't diving into Krav Maga. I made easy, small steps. Then started crushing it.

My motorcycle goal was a hard one. My excuse was always "I don't have the money." But I scheduled the written test and found a riding school and the total cost. I gave myself a timeline for putting aside the money, and taking a riding course. When I had the deposit saved, I booked a weekend I should have the full amount saved by. I forced myself to 'make it happen.' On the second day of my motorcycle course, I started crying on my way to the lesson. I was angry and scared that I wasn't learning fast enough. I was scared of failing the test at the end of the day. I was scared I looked foolish and incompetent. When I pulled into the lot, one of the other students just looked at me, wrapped their arms around me and listened to my fears. Then told me everything was going to be ok. They offered positive support. I just let myself be raw with a complete stranger. I let myself be scared. My instructor looked me in the face and said "You have spent less than 8 hours riding a motorcycle. Less than 24 hours ago - you had never ridden a motorbike. You are doing amazing. Don't be so hard on yourself." Again, positive support from random people. I was hearing the words I needed from those around me to know that it was ok to struggle but that it was important to keep pressing forward. It was ok to be scared, it wasn't ok to give up. I also got a reminder that normal people aren't looking to prey on your vulnerability.

Same goes for this book. Which I had to do on my own. No one was keeping tabs on me. I didn't have instructors or comrades cheering me on. I had to listen to my own internal voice of support and encouragement. Every chapter, every tool, every draft helped me feel capable; helped me feel confident. I schedule time for myself to write. I make timelines and set mini goals for completing chapters. I choose what my success looks like and I make it realistic. I have no idea if I'll get published. I have no idea if people will want to pay for it. I have no idea if it will be helpful to others.

But that's not the point. The success is writing it. The success is determined by my matrix. I own and design my framework for success. I choose where I draw the lines of 'good enough' and 'fucking awesome.'

I don't do this to 'feel good.' Feeling 'good' is so vague. Heroin can make someone feel 'good.' So can going for a jog. I don't do this to feel 'better.' Having a glass of wine (or 6) can make someone feel better than they did earlier in the day. So can cleaning your entire house.

Doing things that make you feel good or better don't improve your feelings of self worth. So now you have a new goal. The level of competence and capability we perceive ourselves to have is what changes how worthy we believe ourselves to be. We need to produce tangible results. I repeatedly created scenarios that allowed me to prove I am a capable and competent person. I built my own self worth.

You can do this as well.

REWIRE YOUR BRAIN

Recap: People raised with toxic parenting participate in a number of addictive behaviors to self soothe. These are pacifiers to alleviate our internal pain and discomfort. People suffering from intergenerational trauma and abuse can participate in self-care activities and gain benefits from doing so. But neither vices, nor self-care that helps us feel 'better' or 'good' will help us build the self worth we are missing from our upbringing. We need to focus on carving out opportunities for us to build self love. It's really hard to 'care' about yourself, if you don't actually love yourself in the first place.

Here are some exercises and tips on how to actively start building that self worth through experiences which reaffirm that you are a competent and capable person:

1) Identify repetitive habits you've formed for making yourself feel 'better' when you feel like shit about yourself: food, curling up in front of the tv, cleaning, shopping, throwing things out, etc

2) Watch yourself start organizing to have that. Start identifying the moments that you begin planning to participate in those activities
   a) Eg: tonight I'm just going to curl up on the couch and 'check out'
   b) Eg: I should clean the bathroom, then vacuum, then get the laundry done when I get home
   c) Eg: I'm going to drink a whole bottle of wine tonight and just let "whatever" go
   d) Eg: On Saturday I'm going to pull everything out of the mudroom and just start chucking stuff I haven't used in a year

3) Plan to do something small to get one of your goals in motion
   a) Eg: before you plunk your ass on the couch, get online and sign up for a that beginners photography course you always wanted to do
   b) Eg: before you allow yourself to start cleaning spend 30 minutes researching how to upgrade your current education to get on a path for the job change you want
   c) Eg: Make a cup of tea and spend one hour making a plan for that personal project you've always wanted to do and then complete the first step
   d) Eg: Clear 3 hours of that Saturday that are entirely devoted to doing something you've always wanted to try, but have never allowed yourself the time or had the 'guts' to do because you're scared you're not going to be perfect at it or it will amount to nothing

4) After you've completed the first step of your goal - have a conversation with yourself:
   a) I've done step one, when can I do step two?
   b) Did I feel I wasted my time? Did I enjoy that?

c)   Did that make me feel successful/capable/competent?

d)   Am I looking forward to the next part?

e)   Does it matter if I fail at this? Can I try again? Can I keep trying?

f)   Who is this important to? (The only answer should be 'you')

g)   If I managed to start this dream/goal/hobbie, I <u>can</u> start any of the other ones I feel like

h)   If nothing has stopped me from pursuing this...is there actually anything in the way of me pursuing my other goals and dreams to whatever degree I decide is possible for me?

Your focus should be participating in things that increase your self worth. Participate in things that make you build an internal foundation of competency, capability and a metric of success that you have designed. This metric needs to be owned and determined by you. Not your mother, not other people, not 'the world.' Just you. No one gives a shit if you do photography as a hobby or if you get paid thousands of dollars. Your mum might. But her opinion - doesn't matter. You decide what success looks like; in every corner of your life.

Then remember: if you succeed 'most days' you're doing pretty great.

Chapter 9
Find Opportunities to be Vulnerable; With Others

Rule #1: Never leave yourself vulnerable.

In a fight.

But when you're not in a fight, you should actually be trying to connect - with people, the world, new experiences, and yourself. The issue here is that we've been raised in a fight. Children who have suffered abuse are in a constant state of survival mode. Fight, flight, or freeze. Emotional abuse from a parent is no different. Having an unloving mother is no different. We grow up learning to put our emotions into a tightly woven steel cage. Our conscious self hangs out around the cage, playing defence - with everything and everyone.

Women raised with dysfunctional mothering have some commonalities built into their protective cages. This includes, but is not limited to: perfectionism, avoiding failure at all costs, always pretending we're fine, having imposter syndrome, not seeking help or support, etc. These are all extracts of having our vulnerabilities preyed on and used against us when we're young.

The rest of the world is not as vicious as your mother. You need to start gaining experiences that allow you to know this is true. Then you need to get addicted to it. We need to rewire our brains to know that, more often than not, being vulnerable renders major rewards. This is for the plain and simple purpose of creating deep, meaningful connections.

These 'connections' are what we have been raised to fear because the first one we were ever supposed to have with our mother is completely toxic. We have no practice, record or experience in having a healthy bond with anyone else. We avoid, sabotage, wreck, and manipulate all of our other relationships.

There are 3 main areas we need to rewire. These 3 areas are strongly connected and interdependent. We need to break the cycle of these bad habits in order to start opening ourselves up to the opportunity of connecting with other, healthy people.

This whole issue is based on emotional fear. Fear of pain, loss, ridicule, social isolation, judgement and most importantly: based on the idea that the rest of the general public will punish our vulnerabilities the same way our mother does.

This. Is. Not. Accurate.

In truth, there is a nice, big, thick line between 2 groups of people: Those who prey on others' vulnerability (toxic people) and people who don't (normal people.) Those who don't prey on someone else's vulnerabilities are people who will empathize, show compassion, connect with you...and will possibly even support and help you. Can you remember the last time you allowed this to happen? Can you remember how scary that was? Can you remember how good it felt when you realized they really weren't going to hurt you? It's incredible, isn't it?

Our goal with this tool is to understand why being vulnerable with others will help you move past your damage, then be able to identify scenarios where we can safely start having these experiences. Following this, we want to develop the confidence in having vulnerability be part of our public selves, even in the face of predatory people.

The 3 Areas to Rewire:

Area 1: Constant Feelings of Inadequacy, Lack of Control, Incapability & Impending Failure

Every tool in this book is actually addressing these main issues. Gaining fluid acceptance of yourself, focusing on your growth instead of your damage, changing your internal voice, setting boundaries - all of these tools are meant to replace these crippling mental models wired by your past experiences. The truth is: everyone feels these things at some point. The difference is that people with a healthy level of self worth only have them sometimes and have tools for overcoming them. Women raised by unloving mothers have low self worth, and these unhealthy ideas consume them daily. This damaged wiring controls them and holds them in a pattern of self sabotage, anger, shame and emotionally protective isolation.

One of the most rewarding parts of life are the relationships we build, which are also termed as our 'connections.' Meaningful relationships are built through deep, genuine connecting. If we refuse to share the parts of ourselves we have been protecting, we will never have the opportunity to experience genuine connections. We cannot build relationships with others, using our stoic, falsely perfect, surface selves. Meaningful or devoted relationships are also very difficult to keep if we are not putting in the work or effort to continue building or maintaining them. We do this by connecting. We connect by sharing vulnerabilities and raw moments.

The ideas you are learning to accept through the tool of fluid acceptance are vulnerabilities that can offer you a chance to connect with someone else.

The attitude you are learning to change through the tool of absorbing growth style knowledge are vulnerabilities that can offer you a chance to connect with someone else.

The self worth you are learning to develop through the tool of practicing competence and capability are vulnerabilities that can offer you a chance to connect with someone else.

The list goes on. These internal expeditions are the exact things that you can start sharing with other people to build bonds. These are not your 'dark parts' which need to be hidden and make you appear damaged or weak. You're 'not perfect' parts are what others will relate to and want to connect about. These are not what scare people off, or make you look broken or undesirable. The pieces of you that are 'under development' are not your flaws. Sharing them with someone else allows an opportunity for you to grow at the same time as someone else; with someone else. To not be alone, even if it's only for a moment.

That is your main take away. You don't have flaws, dark parts, or damaged areas. You have areas of yourself under development. Those are the pieces to use when genuinely connecting with other people. Especially when you change your attitude to those parts of yourself being 'under development.' This is what allows room for you to see progress. A flaw feels permanent. A section of yourself under development, no matter how slow or messy, has potential. It's progressive. Which is actually powerful, as well as empowering. Leading us to our next part of the cycle to break.

Area 2: Being Honest

- *I'm just not_____ enough.*
  (Patient, smart, skilled, good looking, dedicated, organized, stable, etc)
- *I stopped caring.*
- *I didn't commit to it enough.*
- *It wasn't a big deal.*

These are the lies we tell ourselves and tell the people around us in order to protect ourselves. We create this shield in preparation for the unsupportive and vicious commentary offered by our mothers when we share with her. Then as a mental model or muscle memory behavior, we just use it with everyone we share with.

We can lie to ourselves in 2 ways:
1) We make the excuse that we are designed a certain way, therefore not achieving something we set out to accomplish was inevitable

2) We falsify a level of control & choice over the failure - claiming that it was, to some degree, on purpose or by choice that we failed

But secretly or subconsciously we know this is not true. Inside we are silently suffering a loss, failure, inadequacy or defeat. These experiences cause everyone to feel some sense of pain, fear, sadness, which can all feel like states of vulnerability.

Lying about how you feel is disingenuous and fake. Lying to yourself and others about your true feelings isolates you. Not only do you feel alone - but you actually become emotionally alone.

You are not sharing.
Which means you are not connecting.

Lying isn't easier than being honest. Just like how smoking isn't easier than not smoking. If you aren't a smoker, it's pretty easy to not smoke. If you haven't made a habit of hiding your true feelings to protect yourself, then it's easy to be honest about them. If lying about your true feelings is a habit for you, changing that habit is what will feel difficult or uncomfortable. But as soon as being honest about how you feel becomes your habit, that will become your 'easy' setting. The trouble is making the switch.

The difficulty is changing the habit.

The reason this change is difficult is because it already feels safe where we are. Hiding and lying about situations and circumstances that provoke your feelings of vulnerability has been your tool to survive in an abusive relationship (with your mother and yourself.) Our goal is to drag your scared little self by the ankle, kicking and screaming - if we have to - into the wild. A place full of people that do not have the slightest interest in eating you alive.

Breaking the habit of lying about our feelings takes constant and continuous work until the new (healthier) habit is formed. If your current habit is lying about how you feel to protect, shield & hide yourself then your new habit will be telling the truth about how you feel to reveal, uncover & expose yourself.

A great way of ensuring our continued participation in changing a habit is organizing the situation to render the results we want. We want to have the activity of being honest about our feelings and vulnerabilities to be a repeatedly positive experience. How do we do this? Seek out people that are in a position already responsible for making this happen. Find people who are 'invested' in making you a stronger person. Counsellors, instructors, teachers, leaders, gurus, and people who actually love you.

These are the people who, not only benefit from you having a positive growth experience - they actually, unselfishly, hope you have one. They are purposefully participating in behavior that is meant to ensure you have a positive experience while doing something new or scary or something that helps you grow.

Your counsellor or therapist can't help you unless you are honest about what is hurting you, making you scared or uncomfortable. It is their JOB to help you. It is also why they chose that profession. They want to help people. But they can't do that unless you are honest with them.

Instructors, teachers, leaders & gurus are in the business of helping people. Everything from skydiving, snorkeling, and horseback riding to creative writing classes, yoga and meditation. These people have made a career out of taking people who start with no knowledge to people who have leveled up. They NEED you to succeed at doing something new, so you'll turn around and tell other people to contact them if they also want to learn that new thing. Not only does their job depend on you coming out with a good experience - they chose that job because they love helping people have that experience. Your growth is their reward.

Area 3: Asking for Help
Scary? Yes. Uncomfortable? Yes. The perfect opportunity for your toxic mother to victimize you? You bet. When you're in any abusive relationship, requesting help is a predator's playground. They utilize the opportunity for any number of super fun and special torture methods. This includes but is not limited to: making sure you 'owe' them something later, taking complete control of the situation for their egotistical benefit, or making you feel small, stupid, incompetent, feeble, or reinforcing the idea that you are dependent on them. So much fun, right?

If this is our repeated experience - why would we keep asking for help? If every time we get into a situation where we either need help or ask for it, we get ourselves into a situation where we experience emotional torment or abuse...why do it?

Again - all together now:
Because the rest of the world is not as vicious as our toxic parents..

Whether you're trying to start your own business, go back to school, plan a kids birthday or crying and need a hug after an exhausting day of work - there is someone that wants to help you. Just to be nice. They don't want anything from you. Helping someone else - is actually the reward in itself. Most people are like this. The vast majority of people just like being nice. It's true. I promise.

As an adult of childhood emotional abuse, you will notice a difference in how you feel about asking for help, depending on the situation and the person. If asking for help doesn't reveal a vulnerability, then anyone from a stranger to a loved one is perfectly fine. Or if we have decided that a certain persons' perception of us doesn't matter, we are fine with uncovering a moment of incapability. But there are moments where it is strictly unacceptable to have a stranger in our midst see us as imcompetant or have a loved one get a peep at us being anything less than superhuman.

This is what shows that the problem lies within us. Regardless of how someone treats you or perceives you when you ask for help - what matters is how it makes us feel. I fully admit to quoting "it takes strength to ask for help." Then treating that behavior like a disease. It's the muscle memory. It's the past experiences. The negative outcome is seared onto the surface.

Again, we need to change what we know. Change the wiring. Alter our design. We need to start organizing experiences for ourselves that repeatedly offer good results from asking for help. What if we start asking for help from people whose job it is to help us?

- The person who works at the grocery store to take us directly to the item we're looking for.
- The person at the tech store to recommend the best camera or computer to buy.
- The server at the restaurant which dish or wine to have.
- The public health nurse on our child's sleeping/waking cycle.

Why not? What's the harm? That's what they are actually there for. That is their area of expertise. And if we don't feel comfortable with their suggestion - we don't have to take it. They don't think less of us. Or they might. But what they think - doesn't matter.

What if you start asking for help when you don't need it? When it doesn't matter if someone says no, or looks at you like you're an invalid? What if you ask for the other person's sake? Ask in order to offer them a chance to feel helpful or useful. Make it not about your needs, make it about offering them an opportunity.

The point is to make it a habit. The point is to break the discomfort. The goal is to make asking for help a nonthreatening activity for you. What if you could get rid of the feeling that someone saying you owe them after they have helped you, as ominous and crushing? What if you could see that as a great excuse to get more time with them? What if you were happy that they were offering you the chance to return the favour?

If you are working on getting better at asking for help it stops being a vulnerability and starts being a skill under development. Which is a place of progression and growth. Then after you've shifted a number of parts of yourself into this category we can start taking a look at the next level up from this.

The Next Level - Predators Beware

<u>Consider the following concept:</u>

You don't have vulnerabilities.

This is where we stretch the idea of <u>'areas under development.'</u> No matter what you believe is 'wrong with you' - there is nothing <u>wrong</u> with you. There is no area for someone else to poke at, pick the scab off of, or make you feel ashamed about.

No matter what situation or person you approach, there is NOTHING for them to prey on, because you have used the concept of fluid acceptance to make the grey zone your bitch. You are a person. You are growing, learning and changing all the time. Every day. Who you ARE is not permanent. You don't have to be impressed or even happy with where you are at right now. You can just be 'ok' or just be 'comfortable.' Which makes it impossible for toxic, shitty people to say or do things that cause you fear and pain.

You don't' always.'
You don't 'never.'
You don't have issues with intimacy/love/attachment.
You don't have problems with depression/anxiety.
You're not a perfectionist or a fuck up.

You 'sometimes.'
You 'maybe.'
You 'might.'
You 'kind of.'
You just haven't 'yet.'

The idea isn't to 'not have vulnerabilities.' The idea is to change your idea about them being a negative thing. It is incredibly powerful to be able to genuinely respond to insensitive comments like a raindrop off an umbrella. This is a high level of self love.

You: "I haven't really had a chance to travel the world yet."
Other person: "I notice that people who haven't traveled have a pretty significant life experience gap."
You get defensive: "Actually there is a long list of exceptional, talented and brilliant people who scarcely left their hometown and still accomplished significant things throughout history!"

Ok. Calm down. Try again.

You recognize that comment isn't about you. That is the other person's judgey, shitty, projection of their own insecurities. People's rejection or criticisms are most often a comment on their own preferences, not an objective analysis of who you are.

"I'll make it happen when I'm ready. I'm just not there yet. But I'm happy with where I've been already and so far."

The first half of this tool or growth process is about changing the pattern of your experiences. It's about having your future experiences involving vulnerabilities replace your previous memories of torment. We want to identify and participate in situations with a high probability of success to gain confidence in behavior that allows us to thrive.

The second half of this tool is maximizing awareness of our level of control. We want to reach a level of evolution where other people's behavior does not determine our experience. How someone else treats you no longer determines how you feel about yourself.

REWIRE YOUR BRAIN

Recap: Being vulnerable is a super power.

Some people teach/support the idea that admitting our own mistakes is hard, difficult, or takes strength. I'm calling bullshit. This can be as easy as you make it. The words "I failed, I made a mistake, I fucked up, I need help" only have as much power and weight as you give them. They are no more difficult to say than any other group of words.

Even Yoda must eat his own words "do or do not, there is no try" when he admits "Jedi do not live in absolutes." The world is not black and white. It never has been and never will be. Change how you see your vulnerabilities. Choose to make them a gateway. Make them an opportunity for you to connect with others, an opportunity for growth; your next great work of art within yourself.

Here are the tips and tools to get started:
1. Stop isolating yourself. Find other people working on those sections of themselves. Seek out groups, activities, clubs that are dedicated to improving that part of themselves. Even online support groups. Focus on moving that part of you from the section of insecurity, and put it under the heading of 'working on it.' Seek out situations and people where being a beginner is supported, making mistakes to grow is encouraged and being perfect isn't the goal.

2. Work on your internal commentary regarding the parts of yourself you feel vulnerable about. Start with changing the actual words and language you use to describe your vulnerability. Start with changing your language about the vulnerability from permanent to transitional words. This is going from 'always &

never' to 'sometimes or kind of.' Follow up with changing the vulnerability from a flaw to a part of you that is in progress.

3. Stop lying to yourself and stop lying to others about being ok. I actually found a bit of humor in the way I was able to break this habit. I started verbally calling myself out on lying.
    a. Friend: How's it going?
    b. Me: Great, yah, everything is pretty good, fine.
    c. Also me: That's a lie.
    d. Me continuing: I've had a tough week and haven't been making it to the gym and I feel pretty frustrated about it.

    It's almost like having a second person in your head openingly calling you out on the lie. Don't let yourself get away with it. You can start with just calling yourself out. "That's not true." Then push yourself to share the truth. That truth is what will offer the opportunity for connection. It gives the other person a chance to relate & share back or offer compassion & support. Those are the building blocks of a healthy relationship.

4. Split your vulnerabilities in half. Figure out which ones you want to work on or change and move them into the 'skills under development' category. Then look at rest and consider taking proud ownership of them.

    Are you tone deaf but love to sing? Fuck it - just do it. And spend time with people who think that's awesome. Are you the person who can never remember the punch line but love making people laugh? Make buddies and team up with someone who crushes the final delivery but is too shy to start it. Have you always felt awkward about how tall you are and hate towering over men on a date? Start dating men who specifically speak out about appreciating an amazon goddess and fucking own it.

    Make lists of all the things your long legs can do that short legs can't. Are you holding deep seeded personal disappointment that you didn't make it through med school? Start volunteering in hospice work, or a women's center and make use of your passion in healthcare.

5. Devote time to finding and repeating the opportunities that offer you positive experiences from opening up. Set a schedule for participating in activities that strengthen your skills under development. Find a group or a person who has an excellent attitude about doing new things. Get involved with new friends that are on a similar journey as you. Pretending that you are 'perfect' caps your ability to grow and become a better person. Pretending you are perfect doesn't group you with other perfect people. Those people aren't actually real. They don't exist.

6. Make it your responsibility to set a good example. When you see others criticize someone else for making mistakes, judging someone for a failure, or preying on someone else's discomfort - stand up for them. Offer the predator the option of apologizing. Offer them a second option for how to speak to or respond to someone who is sharing a vulnerability. THEN remember that you can do that for yourself as well. You can defend yourself. You do not have to offer yourself up as a victim. You can stop having 'vulnerabilities' by remembering that you are human and there is no such thing as perfect.

Chapter 10
Learn to Repair

A significant gap in the building of ourselves when raised by an unloving mother is the ability to repair after conflict. All of the tools we use following a conflict are twisted versions of typical tools for healthy repair. This makes it extremely painful to have relationships with other humans.

In the toxic mother-daughter dynamic, there is only ever one winner after a fight. How an abusive mother wants to organize that will be dependant on her emotionally abusive mothering style. But no matter what - you're not the winner. Being raised by anyone abusive yields similar survival coping mechanisms. Our tools used to keep our relationship with our mother are actually feeding their ability to continue torturing us.

In addition to this, we don't know how to repair fights we have with ourselves. We don't know how to apologize to ourselves, or to offer ourselves forgiveness. This becomes excruciating to live with. We find it impossible to look at ourselves and say "You're right, that didn't turn out well. It was a mistake. I forgive you. I'll work on not doing that again/anymore."

We need to change our reaction to relationship conflicts; inside and outside of ourselves. There are other options to how they can play out. We have the power to choose what happens after someone hurts us, or when we hurt someone else, or when we hurt ourselves. We don't need to be afraid of showing people that a bond, boundary, promise or level of respect has been damaged or broken. It doesn't make us weak. It doesn't mean that we, as a person are damaged and broken. It also doesn't give someone power over us.

Repair is not a moment of weakness uncovered. Repair is an opportunity to build. We are highlighting an area that we believe could be better. Our past experiences with our mothers have taught us that this is highly dangerous. But we were already participating in this process from a place of toxicity. Developing self respect, self worth and self confidence can help in your ability to repair with others and yourself. It also becomes a cycle of developing strength. Every time you succeed at repairing, you will find more strength in who you are.

Repairing With Other People
Being able to repair is an essential part of having healthy relationships with people (and yourself.) The funny thing is, even if you weren't raised by an emotionally abusive parent - you're still probably not very good at repairing. This is simply the cosmic humor of

being human. Repair requires a few essential things; which are the exact things we toss out the window when we get in a fight or argument with someone we love.

- Repair requires empathy; an understanding or compassion for the feelings/perspective of the other person involved.
- Repair requires taking responsibility for your half.
- Repair requires a desire to stay connected.

When someone hurts our feelings, crosses our boundaries or makes us feel threatened we are not in a mindset to be doing any of those things. We are in survival mode. We are focused on protecting ourselves. Being able to take a deep breath, exercise some emotional intelligence and work your way to a solution requires squeezing out a higher level of thinking from most people. We dig around in our tool box and start the process of repair. We assess whether or not we want to keep the relationship, and to what extent. We attempt to figure out what the miscommunications are. We try to see things from the other person's point of view. We start by just saying 'sorry.' There are all sorts of healthy tools to start getting back on the right track when we fight with a loved one (or anyone.)

The problem with being raised by an abusive parent is that even when you see those tools and try to exercise them - not everyone in the fight is playing fair.

A fight and repair with an unloving/abusive/narcissistic mother looks something like this:
1) They either feel threatened or find an opportunity to feed themselves
2) They prey on or provoke you
3) You use your defence mechanisms and react
4) They manipulate the situation to look like your fault
5) They create emotional punishment
6) You feel shame, guilt, responsibility for the conflict
7) You grovel, apologize, reconcile (or do what you 'think' is repairing)
8) They retain power in the relationship and continue lording over you

In other words: your mum does or says something shitty, you share feelings of that hurting you, she makes it your fault and you put in all the effort to smooth out the relationship to keep it. Utter bullshit.

True repair requires empathy; something that abusers do not often offer. Being raised by a dysfunctional mother doesn't provide opportunity to learn how to make up after a fight in a healthy way. An abuser in a relationship cannot be wrong. Which leaves no room for empathy. The experiences of abuse victims in 'arguments' is that they are never right, they never win and the fight is never felt to be truly fair. Therefore this is false reconciliation.

When we approach a disagreement with our mothers, we use one of our reptilian responses; fight, flight or freeze. It's all we have access to. You are just trying to survive the battle. Repeatedly being involved in unhealthy argument and conflict patterns with our mothers creates our emotional muscle memory. So when we have a fight with anyone else, we experience the same response mechanisms and usually practice the same behavior.

Or - we cut that person out. We do this because we know that repair means grovelling, being wrong or losing power in the relationship. We look at a relationship or connection and actually assess whether or not it's worth keeping. If we fear being vulnerable to that person, we will cut and run, rather than have to go through the torture of the 'repair.' Which we assume will look and feel exactly like the toxic, manipulative and painful process of when we do it with our mothers. Why would we go through a process that allows one more person to have power over us?

This is where a significant amount of our sabotaged relationships come from. Even when we see conflict approaching we will choose to set that relationship ablaze before even considering going through a process of vulnerability, and repair. We would prefer being hated, than seen as fallible. It's too scary.

This is the hiccup: everyone else on the planet will not treat you the same way your mother does.

Here is the key: being able to repair exercises integrity. To behave with integrity shows strength of character. When we choose to act with integrity and identify our behavior as being honest, strong, nobel, mature, responsible - we are participating in behaviors that build self worth.

When we participate in repair, conflict resolution, admitting mistakes, accepting apologies - we are participating in vulnerable moments with other humans that connect us, teach lessons and build strength. We need these moments to prove to ourselves that we can fall and recover. That we are worthy; of love, forgiveness, esteem, compassion, kindness & respect. Respect being a big one. Apologizing to someone else is showing you respect them. Requesting an apology or communicating boundaries is participating in respecting yourself.

Repairing is a tool & skill we need to order to identify and build healthy relationships with other people and ourselves.

Repairing With Yourself

Now consider when you are in a conflict with yourself. We know from the previous chapter of 'Take Ownership of Your Internal Voice' that we can speak to ourselves in horrible ways. Can you even count how many times you've made a mistake, failed, got mad at yourself or done something accidently and refused to forgive yourself? You refuse to accept an apology to yourself. You don't participate in a healthy relationship with yourself. You are your own abuser. Then at different times, your other half either takes the blame (and the shame) or cuts you out. Can you walk yourself through different times when you've done this?

Example: Something didn't go as planned? Getting a new job, getting dumped, failing a course, procrastinating on completing a home project, went out and got wasted when you said you wouldn't?

1) You blame yourself and take that blame:

It was your fault and you know it. You just weren't good enough, you made all the mistakes, didn't do the right things. You tell yourself you fucked up, you admit it and you take that on. It's no one's fault but yours. You shame yourself into a ditch and tell yourself it's because you're incapable of whatever it was that you screwed up.

Or

2) You don't want to pick that fight with yourself:

So you get wasted, shut off your internal voice, distract yourself for a few days, decide it didn't even matter, and you choose to never think about it again. You lock it away in a vault, pretend it doesn't exist. You binge eat or starve yourself, you get obsessed about working out, or fill your schedule so much you don't have time to reflect to gain insight.

We don't know how to apologize or accept an apology within ourselves. This is horrible for 2 reasons. We are treating ourselves with a lack of respect and we are telling ourselves that we are not worthy of an apology.

This
> **is**
>> **bullshit.**

You are the first person you should apologize to.

You are the FIRST person you should set boundaries with.

Having self confidence, self esteem, self awareness, self worth - all of this is part of being comfortable with yourself, your choices, your actions...and - your mistakes. Give yourself room. Not just some room. Give yourself a whole mansion, a castle, a planet....give yourself a universe of space. Use fluid acceptance as your grey zone guide. Throw the word 'sometimes' around like a bowl of glitter at a 6 year old's princess party.

Choose to be worthy of your own forgiveness. Have the integrity to apologize to yourself for making mistakes, failing, falling down, not making it, fucking things up. Then have the compassion to forgive yourself. Then make a plan to reconcile with yourself. Choose the path that you are going to walk, with yourself, to be okay with who you are and what you're doing. No one deserves your respect or love - more than you do. If you're having a hard time doing that - go back to chapter 7 and start finding things that make you feel competent and capable.

There is nothing 'wrong with you' for making mistakes. But it is unhelpful to avoid the uncomfortable process of repairing with yourself. You are worthy of forgiveness - if you choose. You have a right to set boundaries for yourself. It's also ok to make mistakes, then correct them. That's what being human is.

REWIRE YOUR BRAIN
Recap: Repairing is difficult for everyone. There are no exceptions to this. It requires humility, vulnerability and empathy; all at a time when we've felt hurt or threatened. What makes this especially difficult for daughters of unloving mothers is the repeated experiences we've had related to repair that don't turn out well. In fact - it's the process that we identify as allowing us to become or remain someone's victim. Even a victim of our own abusive behavior, as we turn it inward.

Our responsibility is to unlearn this. Repairing takes confidence, strength, and integrity. It is also a process that builds our internal levels of self worth as we prove to ourselves that we can take ownership of our choices and actions. In addition, we practice fluid acceptance by giving people we have relationships, as well as ourselves, some room for growth and change.

Repairing is scary as fuck. But if you break it down into teeny tiny baby steps - it's gets so much easier.

When repairing with others:

1) Understand there is no timeline for repair.
Unless you randomly die, it is not too late. You have every right, opportunity and potential to apologize, repair, or set a boundary with anyone; at any point in time that you want. Whether its 5 minutes after the uncomfortable silence has started or 5 years since the situation happened.
There is NOTHING stopping you from starting your half of the repair with someone. If they've moved away, live on the other side of the planet, blocked your number, deleted you as a Facebook friend. There is nothing stopping you from writing a letter,

email, text, or leaving a voicemail or showing up on their doorstep or at their work like a psycho. There is no amount of time or space that prevents you from initiating repair. It's all in your head. Take your "I can't" attitude and shove it where the sun don't shine.

2)   Stop on your side of the line.
       You only have control of your half of the situation. You will never know how someone will react to your initiation of repair. Can you see the future? No. In fact - your ideas about how someone 'might respond' are not only possibly incorrect - they're fucking useless. They are not helpful in this process. Your assumptions about 'how' they will respond to you either saying sorry or expressing a boundary that you didn't enjoy having them cross - is not where you should be putting your energy. How they 'might' react, should not determine what you think is the best course of action for you.

3)   Establish your own comfort zone.
       You have every right to share or not share as much as you're comfortable with when repairing. You don't owe anyone a 'whole truth.' That's not required in repair. Have clarity with yourself about what you are either asking for or offering.
       If you are requesting repair by expressing that someone hurt you - tell them what you are looking for moving forward. They will choose what they will participate in.
       If you are offering an apology - you can choose how much you're willing to share regarding your actions and behavior.
        Nothing is better or worse. There is no guide, no rubric, no typical outline. Make it genuine, make it honest and own it. It's yours. Just because you're 'giving' the apology to someone, doesn't mean you should be making it look a certain way for them. You're the one making it. It's your creation. And it's meant to express 'you.' Same goes for a boundary. That's 'yours.' It needs to be something that you're proud to put out into the world and believe in.

4)   Nothing is permanent.
       You are allowed to change your mind about anything - any time you want. You are allowed to reconsider, go back and ask questions, start from ground zero, back up, take a detour. Nothing is set in stone. Do not be paralyzed by your choices, or someone else's choices. If you apologize or express a boundary - feel free to take it back or change it. Life is fluid and ever changing. So are you, as a person. And so are other people.
       You can mean every word you say, at the time that you say it. Then you can learn, grow, change and not feel or think the same things at a later time. That's just life. It's ok offer an apology and set a boundary at the same time. It's ok to do it separately. It's even ok to take them both back if you really feel like it. Don't feel crushed by the stone you think your words will be set in.

5)   Recognize what repairing is for (and what it isn't for.)
       After reading about learning to be vulnerable with people, building deep genuine bonds should be something you start learning to do. Being able to repair is a huge part of

that journey. Repairing is a hard process that requires a lot of tools (most of which we didn't get help developing.) It requires exercising our boundaries, understanding our unique values around forgiveness, being vulnerable, and fluid acceptance.

Repairing is a part of building connections with people. There are no relationships in our lives that are flawless or always smooth. Over time, in order to keep them and make them deep, we need to resolve conflicts and show both compassion and humility. This is how you create a tribe or community. Most of all - repairing should empower you. It should make you feel stronger.

If you go through a process of repair with someone and it makes you feel weak; you are probably participating in another toxic relationship. Repairing is not about offering or re-granting permission. Repairing does not mean that things are allowed to continue as they were before. That's how the damage was done in the first place.

6) Treat your repair like a gift.
First - make sure its from the heart. Make it meaningful and represent how you feel about your relationship between you and that person. Make it honest. Once you offer it to someone else; you have no control of what they choose to do with it. You have to be ok with this. It's the nature of the beast. They can return it, smash it, give it to someone else, be surprised, be thankful, cry, laugh, get more angry. That's not your choice. It's also not the point. If you're offering an apology, give it to them because you want them to have it. No conditions apply. Whether you're offering an apology or setting a boundary, hand it to them and step back. They can interact with your gift however they like. If they cherish it - great! Enjoy that. If they toss it around like a piece of crap, don't stand there and watch. Just be somewhere else.

Repairing with yourself is a little bit different.

1) Be the most annoying, persistent, relentless lover, salesman, child with a sweet tooth, ever.
Start that conversation immediately. Do not ignore yourself. Write that letter. Take yourself out for coffee and have that hard talk. Do not leave yourself alone. Tell yourself over and over again how sorry you are. Open your heart and forgive yourself as though you're the Dalai Lama. If you don't do this - the self hate, anger, discomfort will consume you. Like it always has. Stop. That.

2) Be as honest and open with yourself as possible.
Don't hide anything. You can't. Admit the pain, bad behavior, mistake, sabotage and dig deep. Develop that deeper connection with yourself by explaining to yourself 'why' it happened. Turn over every leaf and cover all your bases. Behaving badly towards yourself doesn't mean you're a bad person. You will be learning how to be the person you want to be, for the entirety of your life.

3) <u>Cross your own boundaries.</u>
      Give yourself a school yard shove. Then make sure you shove back. You have total control over your participation in this. It's ok to push yourself to see what happens. Drag in weird concepts, play thought experiments. Imagine who you want to be at the end of the process and figure out how to fill in the path to get there. Or uncover your path as you go. You decide how this plays out. You are responsible for both sides of establishing that you broke your own boundary and learning how to respect it.

4) <u>Work at that repair until it's permanent.</u>
      That could take a few days, it could take a lifetime. That's totally fine. It's the attitude about repairing with yourself that matters. Repair is about building relationships and the most important one you have is with yourself. If you're not solid from the ground up, you have the potential to crumble. It's ok to sway in the wind a bit. But approach every crack in your structure like you're building a legacy. Fortify that shit. You have to live with yourself until the end of your days.

Practice, practice, practice.

Practice doesn't make perfect.

Practice builds muscle memory.

      Your goal with this tool is to have confidence in creating, keeping, building and deepening <u>healthy</u> relationships. Everyone else you're doing this with is on a learning path too. Some of them are farther along. Some of them have no idea how to do this. Some of the moments and people you choose to repair with will blow up in your face. That's reality. But other times - it will allow you share a connection with someone (or yourself) that builds a positive memory and experience. The more of these we participate in, the more we thrive.

When Repair Should Not Take Place
      If you, at any point, or for any reason, feel or experience someone using a repair situation as a way to victimize you - stop.

Do not take on more than your half.

<u>If you are setting a boundary or requesting an apology:</u>
1) All you're doing is stating what you are willing to participate in, accept or tolerate in your life.
2) You are not not telling them what to do, how to behave or making demands on them.
3) Your boundaries are your choice. They are valid.
4) You felt they were crossed. Regardless of how they see their side of the situation.

If you are making an apology or requesting forgiveness:
1) This does not put them above you.
2) You don't OWE them any more than you are willing to give. Their forgiveness should not have conditions. It's their right to communicate that crossing their boundaries in the future can have consequences. But continued punishment after forgiveness or requiring you to grovel is toxic.
3) You do not have to admit to, take on, or be blamed for anything more than you're sure about.

Anyone who will not participate in the repair process in a healthy way with you can be walked away from. You can't change the people around you, but you can change the people you allow to be around you.

Chapter 11

Force Transformation from Insight

This chapter was originally titled "Rewrite Your Past (in 2 ways.)" It took me a while to come back to it and think about the essence of this tool. First of all - I didn't use these exercises to feel differently about my past, as the original title suggested. I used them to adjust my perspective of my present self and to find strength to move forward in my life, in a healthier and more empowered way.

Second - looking into your past, or gaining insight - is only helpful if you're going to utilize that information. These exercises are meant to help us analyze the toxic cycles we have been stuck in due to our emotionally abusive upbringing. Then pull that cycle apart and change how we operate. We are transforming our path to allow us to move forward with higher self worth and improved lifestyle habits. The insight we gain must be 'put to work.'

The 2 exercises below are ones I found to be really helpful for my recovery from gaslighting and being raised by a narcissistic/emotionally unavailable mother. The first one needs the handwritten aspect. The act of writing it out, long hand, on paper unearths more than one would expect. The exercise comes from the book *Mother's Who Can't Love* by Susan Forward. The second exercise I developed through a discussion with a friend. I later came back to the previously mentioned book by Susan Forward and rediscovered a similar exercise about uncovering toxic ideas we were raised with. This exercise can simply be a mental process, but can also be written out or made into a chart on a computer.

The goals of these tools cannot stop at gaining insight. They need to be followed up with a change of current self image. Use the awareness they provide to inform your future choices on becoming who you want to be. Allow them to free you from the bonds and labels of who you thought you were.

The first exercise can be very emotional and requires a free flow of thought.

The second is very logical, methodical and leads into Chapter 8.

Exercise 1: Mom - you shouldn't have...

This writing exercise has a purpose of giving a person the opportunity to tell their mother what they feel she did wrong. What actually happens though, is (often) an uncovering of deeper emotional issues that are extremely hidden in lost memories. For me, this exercise finally helped me find out why or where I had gotten the idea that there was something 'wrong with me.' It can be very powerful to find the source of why you are constantly self sabotaging, malfunctioning, and struggling to get a grip on life.

The exercise begins with writing one of the following sentence starters:
- *Mum, you shouldn't have...*
- *Mum, it wasn't right when you/how you...*
- *Mum, this is what you did to me...*

I chose the last one, and I'm offering the full, unedited writing that I did, while sitting in a Nissan dealership waiting for my car, summer of 2018.

Mum, This is what you did to me: You lied to me. You lied to me about myself and the way the world worked. Not by accident. On purpose. You wanted me to see the world and myself a certain way in hopes to contour how I behaved and the choices I would make. You encouraged me to hold in and control my emotions. You did this on purpose because YOU couldn't handle processing them and you did it to maintain composure of our family's image. I bet seeing someone else's emotions in a wild and uncontrolled state threatened you beyond belief. You did this to me to protect and save yourself. You did this to an innocent child - your own child - you selfish bitch. You hardened a child's heart to save your own fragile self. Fuck you.

You made me feel like my intense emotions were wrong and shameful and needed to be kept a secret. That they needed to be contained.

You reminded me often that I was perfect or exceptional by design - most often when you were shaming me for making a mistake or having a flaw. That you didn't understand where that was coming from. You told me that my upbringing, parenting, raising and what life was offering me was so far and above what others have that me having flaws was bizarre and confusing for you. How am I supposed to explain this to myself as a child still learning about the world? Still learning about myself?

You have never told me you were proud of me. Then I later learned that all you ever told other people about me was how proud of me you were and how well I was doing. You would brag about me, but never share with me that pride you had about me. When I confronted you - you screamed at me "You need that?!"

I could have hit you - like a mother slapping a disrespectful child. I could have pummelled you - like a wild animal defending its honor and devouring its enemy. I could have wrapped my searing fingertips around your throat and slowly squeezed the pipe your lungs need to access oxygen. I would have loved to see the fear in your eyes as you question how far I will go. Then I would give my thumbs one final push of pressure and hear the snap or pop of your larynx.

I still minimize the shitty things (you) did. I make the horrific excuse that is wasn't a big deal, other mothers must have done similar things. I only uncover them as I look at my options of how to treat my own daughter and realize your behavior is the furthest from what I think is 'loving.' It is my job to make her feel special. The most special to me, especially. You made it your job to make sure I felt conflictingly unspecial.

Am I special or not? Special to certain people? That's the club you create - those are your 'loved ones.' The people you bring in close to yourself and trust.

I remember when I finally decided to cut my hair for the first time in 11 years. I had 3.5 feet of blonde virgin hair half way down my thighs. I had either just come back from or was just on my way to a therapy appnt. I was living at home with you and dad between my first and second year of university. I was looking in the mirror in the bathroom upstairs and knew you were close outside the door. "Mum, I'm going to cut my hair today."

"<u>You're</u> going to cut your hair or you're going to get your hair cut?"

"<u>I'm</u> going to cut it."

You furrowed your brow and let out a short disappointing sigh or grunt then walked away in silence. Nothing after that. I remember years later when Ryan and I were over for our divorce party. We were at your sister Chris's and you reached out and caressed my healthy shoulder length blonde hair, supposedly admiring it's fullness and length. I had already started drinking that day. I remember slapping your hand away - your attempt at an affectionate touch was so foreign. I firmly asked "Could you please not touch me?"

And you know what - fuck you.

The time I cut it for the first time in 11 years was a transformative and freeing choice. You did nothing to engage with me about that transition. You inquired about nothing.

And when I came over to the mainland to have a fucking divorce party - you asked nothing. You didn't try to talk to me about how I was feeling or doing. You chose this moment in my life to share your interest in how I looked. After 2 decades of never showing any positive interest in my appearance. I know you purposefully ignored my beauty growing up to not encourage any sense of vanity. Even worse you sex shamed me. You enforced the idea that if I received negative commentary or reactions from people in regards to sexuality or sexual behavior that it was my fault. My fault. Fuck you. At the point in my life when I had finally started growing out of the damage you caused my self image - you offer praise for my naturally pleasing attributes. FUCK YOU.

While growing up - I was bullied a lot. You told me this was because I was different and unique. That the other kids had a difficult time with me and understanding me or felt threatened by me because of my nature. That I was out spoken and more mature and had different ideas or was creative. That's why I got picked on. You never said it was ok for the other kids to treat me that way but you gave me the reasoning that the cause for their mean and exclusionary treatment was 'me' and my unique personality. That 'who I was' as a person was why I got bullied.

Not because other kids are shitty or because they probably get picked on at home or because they haven't been taught how to deal with their own insecurities or their parents let that happen at home. You explained that people fear and are uncomfortable with what's different and that's true. You tried to give me advice and pointers on how to ignore it or protect myself. But you explained it in a way that I was the cause for people to react that way. My way of being and my natural self was the provocation for people's negative reaction towards me.

It took me until my mid twenties to learn that people's reactions are a reflection of themselves. It's a comment about who they are inside - not the person they are reacting to. There are so many people who respond in a positive way to who I am.

****

Although what is written doesn't directly lay out the epiphany or emotional transformation I gained from the exercise, it launched the exploration. Some of the writing is just angry memories. Other parts of the writing has memories and explanations to my mother about why her actions were hurtful or wrong. This brought many hidden points to the surface. It reveals the framework underneath the discomfort and trauma in the memories. In this particular case I was able to find where my deep sense of personal shame came from.

Conversations with my mother when I was young developed the idea that I was unique and different compared to most people and that's why I experienced negative social responses. I remember having discussions where she taught me that people fear or dislike what is unfamiliar, unknown or different. Every negative social experience I had growing up reinforced the idea that openly being my natural self was the cause. *If only I had responded like a normal person. If only I could have hidden or stopped short of doing it the way that felt natural to me. I wouldn't have been criticized, judged, hated, rejected. If I had just acted like everyone else (or kept my mouth shut)... I would have succeed in this situation.*

I realized through this exercise that every failure/rejection which caused me to crawl inside and blame myself came from the idea that who I was naturally, as a person, was why I experienced rejection. I spent most of my teenage years being aggressively different as a defence tactic. I rejected the world, before it could reject me first. I sabotaged and set ablaze opportunities for success to avoid presupposed 'failure by design.'

After writing this I was able to apply another piece of 'self-help' knowledge I had learned in early University. During that time, I was dating a lot and learning about 'choosing relationships.' Through conversations with other people looking for love, I came across a very relieving piece of psychology: A person's rejection of you is not a comment about you - it is a statement of their own preferences.

Writing this letter helped me recognize the amount of rejection I was experiencing towards myself. My preferences (just like ideas about success) were designed by my mother. How she explained the world, behaved in it and reacted to it communicated her preferences. Many of which showcased zero tolerance for being criticised, at fault, or imperfect in any way. Operating with those preferences lead to large amounts of self hate. In other words: shame.

Shame: *an unpleasant self-conscious emotion typically associated with a negative evaluation of the self, withdrawal motivations, and feelings of distress, exposure, mistrust, powerlessness, and worthlessness.*

From that point - I chose to change my preferences. It was bizarre how passionately I loved the weird, the wild and the unapologetically free parts of the world. Yet, when these parts of myself would shine, the compliments shocked me or hold no weight. While the criticisms would crush me and send me into furries of self flogging. But those were not my preferences. They were my mother's. And I decided to stop having them. I decided to show favorable preference for who I was naturally. I chose to start loving who I am, determined by my own rubric.

More importantly, I applied internal and external locus in a more balanced way. My failures were not about 'who I am.' They are about how I participated in a situation as well as the elements involved. Everytime a circumstance develops poorly, I no longer blame my nature and design. I look at what could be better or different next time; both with the role I choose to play and all other factors involved. It is ok to fail, and it's ok to try again; but it's not ok to give up.

Exercise 2: Lies Our Mothers Tell Us.

This exercise is actually kind of fun...or should be. It's about identifying ideas you have about the world that come from your mother which are false or warped. It has 2 positive effects:

1) Gives you opportunities to see the world in a new way, opening doors for growth, adventure and self love
2) It closes the door on your mother having emotional control over you as you uncover her bullshit

This one is great because you can actually laugh out loud while doing it. Literally throw your head back and cackle like an evil mastermind. In public or private - that's your comfort level to determine. As you tear apart ideas and hold them up for analysis, you'll find the ridiculous nature of your mother's gaslighting, emotional abuse and convoluted/delusional impression of the world. While you're doing this, recognize that discrediting information a person shares puts them in a permanent category of a bullshitter. Once you realize that most of what they say doesn't hold any weight or mean anything - it becomes very easy to not take anything they share into consideration. It becomes a joke.

It helps to first understand the difference between implicit (implied) and explicit (direct.) There are tons of things we hear our parents 'say.' Then there is a whole boat load more of concepts we absorb through their actions and behavior. It's important to dig around and uncover both.

Discrediting both implicit and explicit concepts from toxic parenting is extremely important to stop the cycle of wasted energy and thought. In gaslighting and emotional abuse, it is very easy to get lost in a tunnel. It is easy for a victim to form the habit of focusing on information coming selectively from their abuser. What they say, how they act and respond becomes our whole world. We forget to include all of the other information available to us to make proportionate comparisons. This micro-environment we are being crushed into by our abuser's false representations keeps us very busy and exhausted. We forget to lift our heads and absorb comparative information from other sources. Sometimes even when it's offered, we find it stressful to include. We know there is a huge list of emotional punishment tactics implemented for defying the reality they are organizing around us.

This needs to stop. Our mothers are not right about everything simply because they are 'mothers.' Having them angry with us is not the end of the world. We are individuals, capable and responsible for deciding how we view the world. Healthy loving parents empower their children to carve their own path and set their own standards for life.

Here is a sample of the Bullshit Breaker Chart:

What mom taught: You must have a relationship with me (your mother.) You need me & you have to put up with me, because I'm your family.
True/False? FALSE!
Why? Share Examples
There are millions of people throughout history that have become successful, capable, good people despite not having relationships with their mothers. Literally billions of people. All over the world. This can be regardless of why there is no relationship (choosing no contact, early death, etc.) Being someone's mother doesn't give you a right to

a relationship with them, especially when they are an adult, and especially if you are a toxic/abusive person.
Bullshit? YES!

What mom taught: If you get negative sexual attention, you're wearing or doing something to provoke it
True/False? FALSE!
Why? Share Examples

      No matter what a person wears, or how they behave, negative sexual conduct represents the perpetrators idea of acceptable behavior, not my provocation. Guys have also cat-called fully dressed women. Showing skin is never an invitation. There is nothing wrong with dressing or behaving sexually for my own pleasure. I can vocalize my displeasure at how I'm being treated, no matter what I'm wearing or doing. What I wear, or how little, does not determine the amount of respect I deserve to be treated with. Women who dress or behave sexually are not 'sluts.' Everyone from the lingerie models in the Sears catalogue to Lady Gaga.
Bullshit? YES!

What mom taught: Moving alone to another country to work for six months is very dangerous. If something happens you will have nothing, and no one to help you.
True/False? FALSE!
Why? Share Examples

      Thousands of young people move to other countries to work, explore and live....every year. Probably every month. They find jobs, make friends, make mistakes, survive, and come home alive. If all of my things get stolen, or I lose my passport or get robbed, I can find my countries consulate, I can find a library and email home for help, I can tell my new boss at my new job and ask for help. I am not 'alone' in another country. Just like in my own country at home, there are safe, friendly, helpful people. If I'm smart, capable and resourceful, I can find solutions to my problems, no matter where I am or what I'm doing. Also - the likelihood of bad things happening to me while living abroad can depend on the energy I manifest and choices I make. "The difference between adventure and ordeal is attitude."
Bullshit? YES!

What mom taught: Your child NEEDS all 4 grandparents in her life. Cutting me out of her life will damage them.
True/False? FALSE!
Why? Share Examples

      I shouldn't even have to dignify this one with a response. The majority of children have grown up and not even been slightly affected by having less than a full set of grandparents. Some kids even get raised with 5 grandparents! And they aren't better or worse people because of it. No kid, ever, wound up in therapy as an adult with the problem "I'm super fucked up because I grew up with 3 grandparents instead of 4. One was dead

already before I was born, and I've struggled with it my whole life." That's not a thing.
Bullshit? YES!

What mom taught:
If you move in with your boyfriend right after highschool you could get pregnant accidentally, decide to keep it and ruin your life.
True/False? FALSE!
You're right - that could happen. I could get accidentally pregnant. I could decide to keep it. But why would that be ruining my life? Does it mean I would never go to university? No. Does it mean I would be an unfit mother because I'm too young? No. Would the rest of the family abandoned me and not help because the child wasn't planned? Maybe some of them would. We don't know that. Would I struggle the rest of my life with money and relationships and hate myself? Only if I choose. Or maybe none of that will happen. There are also a number of other ways I could ruin my life...you just watch.
Bullshit? YES!

What mom taught:
My siblings and I mostly raised ourselves so we didn't get any intergenerational abuse passed down to us. Which means I didn't pass any issues onto you kids while raising you.
True/False? FALSE!
Why? Share Examples
Raising yourself growing up - is abuse. Its neglect, and has a number of emotional repercussions that carry into adulthood. Your mother is NOT PERFECT. This is impossible. What is worse, is not being able to reflect on one's own life and admit or even identify that there were problems. Anyone who claims to be flawless or attempts to portray themselves that way is seriously sick.
Bullshit? YES!

****

The problem with the ideas and statements above is they actually affect us when the situations come up. They are meant to. They especially affect us while still in the grasp of that relationship. They pull at our heart strings, make us feel guilty, back us into a corner. Our bullshit radar is clouded by years of abuse and unloving parenting. We need to wipe the fog off that window and get a better look at the sharp reality beyond.

The best way to clear that fog is to get time and space away from your mother. You need room to take a deep breath and think calmly about the implicit and explicit ideas she had raised you with that cause you anxiety and stress. Once you can start debunking her past and current bullshit in a separate environment, you will get practice and be able to establish it more immediately.

REWIRE YOUR BRAIN

Recap: Take into consideration that your unloving mother might not know any better than what she raised you with. These concepts were passed on to you from a place of fear, pain and her own unhealed toxicity. It's not her 'fault' but it was her responsibility. Now it's yours. It's your responsibility to pull apart the information about life that you were offered, and make your own choices. It's your responsibility to break the cycle of abuse and toxic concepts. You cannot stop at 'knowing thyself.' To recover and thrive, you must press forward.

1. When analyzing these exercises afterwards, don't focus on blame.
    a. Focus on recovery. The energy is different.
    b. Be self focused - not focused on your mother. The time for pointing a finger is over. You can't change her. But through digging into your own reactions, responses and memories, you can make discoveries that will help you change yourself. It's the only thing you truly have control of.

2. Keep track of your discoveries:
    a. If something stands out - create an affirmation about it. Put it on a post-it note. Write it on the mirror you look in every morning. Have a giant wall decal made and put it up in the living room. Whatever you need to remind you of the change you've discovered within yourself - do it. Commit to it. Roll around in it like the softest blanket you've ever felt. You've earned it.
    b. If you make another discovery that contradicts the one you previously committed to - Great! Tear down the last one, put up the new one! Or don't! Put them beside each other. Learn that both can be true. Or one leads to the other. Or different lessons are needed at different times. Grow your mind, change your mind, live in the grey zone! Everything is fluid! The grey zone is your bitch!

3. Build on your discoveries:
    a. Use the Growth Style Knowledge tool and start exploring topics around what you've discovered. Start finding ways to surround yourself with positive, supportive encouragement for the recovery you've just opened yourself up to. Find books, videos, seminars, or conversations with strangers about new concepts that you've unleashed. Make connections, build bonds, don't be afraid of being wrong or new or confused. It's ok. Everything is ok. The world is not full of people like your toxic mother. Set healthy boundaries, collect healthy relationships and form healthy connections.

4. Find supportive mantras. Whether you are still involved with your mother or not, it helps to be prepared. When she says things, or you think things - be ready with:
    i. I don't think that's true
    ii. That's just your opinion

   iii. That's only one side of the story
   iv. I should ask someone else about that
   v. That sounds like bullshit!

5. Use the 70/20/10 Rule.
 a. 70% of your thought process should be on what's in front of you and who you want to be 'right now.' Make choices, have relationships, and have words coming out of your mouth that are congruent with what 'you' believe.
 b. 20% of your thoughts should be focused on who you are working on being. There should always be a piece of you or a piece of your time used to look at the better person you can be tomorrow.
 c. 10% of your time should be used on looking back and gaining insight. If you spend too much time looking backwards, you can't see where you're going.

The point is to get off the analytical hamster wheel. The goal is transformation after insight.

Chapter 12

Trust in the Majority
Not Your Mother

You've never been an organized enough person to succeed at that. You don't look good in that colour. You always pick deadbeat men. Your body shape has always been a bit awkward. You were never smart enough for university. You always sabotage your relationships. You've never been good at being on your own.

People don't talk about those things. Women who dress like that bring it on themselves. People don't appreciate aggressive women. That's a second-rate career position. No one is going to help you with that. Other people don't care about things like that. That doesn't turn out well for any body.

This tool is a continuation of the Bullshit Breaker Chart from Chapter 11. It is also a supporting tool for Take Ownership of Your Internal Voice from Chapter 6. This section is going to be especially helpful for those who have suffered gaslighting. When you are unknowingly a victim of gaslighting, almost your entire world is organized by your abuser. They force your dependency on the reality they deliver. I imagine it's similar to being raised in a cult - but you're the only member.

(Wait - It's totally like a cult. If you mother has her claws dug into anyone in addition to you...that's the dysfunctional cult. Don't worry, she will not Jones Town you - she needs to keep you all alive to feed herself. Though sometimes you may feel like offing yourself just to get out.)

The greater challenge comes when you become aware that you've been gaslit. You no longer trust the person who was contouring your perception of events and your environment, and you have been conditioned to not trust your own version either. As I went over in Chapter 3, this can be shocking. You don't trust your own reactions, feelings, perceptions and judgement of anything; and you certainly don't trust the suggestions of others. (After recognizing the gaslighting, I actually went through a few months of feeling I had lost my identity. I went through a time of questioning all of my memories, not trusting if any of my past was 'real.' I lost all grounding and trust in my ideas about who I was and how I got to where I was in life.)

The best tool I could develop for this is continually tapping into <u>HEALTHY</u> external sources to get a broad spectrum. When a large group of people decide on 'what is' and are able to support this with evidence and facts, you have a consensus. This is what helps us define our world and is as close to objective knowledge as we can get.

Reality - the world or state of things as they actually exist.

Reality needs to be as objective as possible. Meaning a 'person' has not put their subjective spin on it. But there are tons of situations where people need to fill in the gaps when no knowledge is presented. This is where the emotional abuse can get exercised, especially with children. Children are dangerously susceptible to filling in the blanks incorrectly, due to lack of experience and understanding.

For example:

Almost everyone can agree on a number of things: when something is blue, what classifies as a tree, if something is wet, etc. These things are objective realities. You can drag them into subjective sections such as navy blue or peacock blue, a tree that's good for climbing or not, or if something is damp or soaked. But there is the original objective reality of it. This is where facts come from: a large group of humans use evidence and logic to agree on objective parts of reality: a colour, a classification of plant, whether or not something has come into contact with liquid. Logic, facts, reality.

Where gaslighting and emotionally immature parenting creates problems is the area that involves subjective thoughts about ourselves and the world around us. Am I a failure? Am I smart? Am I good looking? Is that a stupid choice? Am I capable of that? Was I being overly sensitive? Is it ok for someone to treat me this way? Is that safe?

When we have an emotionally abusive caregiver we have a number of subjective ideas reinforced that are misrepresented as objective. We are taught concepts (implicitly & explicitly) about the world and ourselves that are not necessarily true. Then as we grow up and expand our social interactions to strangers, acquaintances, work colleagues and partners we hear a lot of conflicting information. Yet even as we receive these other perspectives, we hold on to the lies we've adopted from our abusive upbringing. This needs to stop.

The best way I found to do this is to outsource to the majority. I had to test every idea I had. When using the Bullshit Breaker Chart I approached trusted friends and talked about these ideas. Rolling the concepts around in your own head will not get you anywhere. The conversations that already drive you mental are the private ones that put you on a hamster wheel in the first place. This hamster wheel is filled with the perceptions your mother has fed you over the years. You just keep running through them, with no exit.

I will offer 2 examples from my own life. One is a body image issue I had, perpetuated further by an 'information gap.' The other was a lot more direct gaslighting, possibly falling into the category of Munchausen Syndrome by proxy.

Long Torso, Short Legs

Growing up my mother often informed me that I had a long torso and that I was shaped like my Aunt Debbie (my father's sister.) There was never an indication as to whether or not this was attractive or complementary. It was just a fact she stated. It came up when looking for shirts, or how a dress fit. We didn't talk about my legs in relation to this but as a young girl I had to fill in the blanks. She also never referred to me as, or directly told me I was pretty, beautiful, or good looking.

Mum says I have a long torso but doesn't say that about my legs. She says nothing about my legs. Her body has long legs and an average length torso. This must mean I have short legs, or shorter than average.

So I spent up to the age of about 25 believing I had disproportionately short legs, especially in comparison to my torso. This was how I viewed myself in dresses, pants, mirrors and pictures. I saw wide hips, dumpy legs, thick thighs. It was just a fact. I just lived with it. If people commented on how tall I was I often responded with a smile "yah, I'm all torso." (Kind of falling into Body Dysmorphic Disorder, if you want to get technical about it...)

In my mid twenties I got a lot more comfortable talking about my body. Meeting other moms and talking about our 'mom-bods' and dating again after my separation, 'body talk' just comes up. I was more open to admitting issues I had and not so afraid to be honest about my insecurities. I was working towards accepting how I was shaped and just being happy with it. Focusing more on what my body was capable of, and not so much what it 'looked like.'

This also opened the door to counter comments. Which were things like "Short legs?! Your legs aren't short! What are you talking about?" When you first hear things like this you can kind of brush it off as people just being nice, or supportive. Women do this with each other all the time. They form community and bonds by being complementary and supportive with white lies. Which is what I thought was happening. But sometimes I would get into the conversation of where that thought came from. After explaining it to a few different curious people I realized what a garbage thought it was. The only person that actually thought I had 'short legs' was me. I went back through photos. I took new photos. I compared the proportions to other people in those photos.

I had spent ages 12 to 25 thinking I had unattractively short legs. All from one particular way my mother spoke to me about my body. The comment itself isn't emotionally abusive. But the repetitive and focused nature of the comment with no other discussions developing around it became extremely damaging over time. With no other discussions about my body with my mother to help fill in the gaps and form a healthy self image, it's easy to get lost. Finding a more accurate self image took over a dozen people not agreeing with me. I now had proof from multiple sources, that my legs were not short and not unattractive. Majority rules. I changed my mind based on a group perspective.

Manic Depressive, Bipolar

My mother and I have very different personalities. She is conventional, introverted, subtle, very emotionally reserved. I am not. I am open, social, intense, passionate and unorthodox. Mix my natural personality with teenage hormones and things look a bit like a WWII battle field. They do with most teenagers though, regardless of personality type.

But my mother - decided I was on the bipolar/manic depressive 'spectrum.' Her sister was diagnosed and so was my cousin, so it was 'in the genetics.' My mother never took me to a professional to have this confirmed though. By the age of 13, she had both me and herself convinced that my emotional outbursts, strong feelings and expressions, times of low moods and depression, obsessive excitement over new experiences - were all part of my manic cycles developing. A condition I would be living with for the rest of my life. Not only had she determined this herself - but she would be the one to help me manage it, the way she thought best.

She was strongly against pharmaceuticals. Her own research determined that anxiety and depression come from a combination of malnutrition, lack of sleep and not enough exercise or activity. Her research showed that depression and anxiety were all a common symptom among low vitamin D, K, B, low Iron or anemia and a number of other nutritional deficiencies. So - she made sure to load me up with vitamins, provide me with natural sleep aids and reminded me to stay active.

This also meant that any time I displayed strong emotions, had a tantrum, felt really depressed, was behaving 'out of control' - I was experiencing another manic episode. Then I would be asked the following:

Have you been keeping up on your vitamins?
Are you getting enough sleep?
Are you staying active enough?

This went on into my early 20s. Every time she could see me struggling, she asked these questions. Every time I got angry with her. Every time I was strongly upset about anything. Every time she decided I was behaving erratically. They were followed with the reminders and warnings of my condition. Whatever craziness I was experiencing was simply being accentuated or blown out of proportion by my permanent hormone/chemical imbalance or mental illness. It was just the result of me not managing my sleep, vitamins and activity levels properly. Nothing was actually wrong in my life. I just wasn't taking my vitamins, getting enough sleep or I should be getting to the gym more.

Until I made the observation of being 'episode free' for 3 years at the age of 22. I was living with my partner that would become my husband and the father of our incredible daughter. He is 13 years older than me, has experienced a huge life; and also watched his cousin be overtaken by mental illness from the time they were children together.

In our first year together he saw me experience grief, disappointment, anger, fear, pride, joy, intense motivation, challenge and reward. He made a cautious approach on that day. "Hun, maybe...you don't have bipolar?"

At the beginning of the relationship, and when we moved in together, I asked for his help and support with this condition. He was kind and diligent about reminding me to take my vitamins and get my sleep. But after some time of living together, he brought this up.

We dug deep on the topic together. He helped me go over the facts. We compared my experiences with clinical reports on bipolar & manic behaviors. We looked at the correlation between finding out about my gluten allergy at age 19 and the life changes that occurred afterward. He shared his experiences of watching his cousin's mental illness develop into adulthood, the variety of personality types he's come across in his life time including people with depression and anxiety issues, and we also talked about how emotionally charged the teenage years can be; for everyone. Also how ineffective 'vitamins, sleep & exercise' are in placating true mental illness.

As I kept exploring the possibility that I didn't have manic depression or bipolar disorder, more evidence confirmed it. Including the concept that during our adolescence is when we begin the process of developing coping mechanisms and tools to handle life's challenges independently. But when our caregivers or other adults are not supportive or present in our lives to help guide us through this process of discovery and development - we can get pretty lost. The more people I spoke to and more questions I asked, the more confident I became in determining what my experiences meant. I collected massive amounts of information from a huge range of sources & people. The broader perspective allowed me to shape a more informed and confident reality for myself.

I wasn't on the mental illness spectrum. I just didn't have a caregiver that was able to help me find and develop coping mechanisms and tools for life. That's all.

Get a Bigger Picture

Your mother's truth is not THE truth. Her reality is a single source and it is not reliable. In fact - it's probably warped as fuck. This can be applied to SO MANY THINGS your mother has directly or indirectly taught you about yourself and the world.

You always downplay your work, skill sets & competency? But other people always comment on how impressive you are.

Traveling alone to do some soul searching is dangerous or a waste of time? People do this all the time and come home alive and happy.

You're too sensitive, overly reactive or emotionally imbalanced? Probably just with your mother because she says horrible, rude, digging comments that would be painful to anyone.

Women who are provocative are disgusting and shameless? Lady Gaga, Madonna, Marilyn Monroe - classy, beautiful, powerful. They're also talented, dynamic and intelligent.

Where you need to go with this is: every time you have something shitty to say about yourself, ask "do other people see/experience/think of me this way?" Furthermore, every time you are scared, uncomfortable, or judgemental about something, ask "is this how the world works/looks for everyone?" But don't just ask yourself - ask EVERYONE ELSE.

Join the Club

People who are victims of emotionally abusive parenting who become high achievers are often masking a deep rooted feeling of being frauds (now known as imposter syndrome.) They know people see them as a stoic lion, but are scared shitless of having this supposed costume torn off them and found to be a cockroach underneath.

Think about the truth of this. People are not so easily fooled. A cockroach in a lion's costume does not become capable of accomplishing a lion's work just because he looks like one. A lion does not ever become a cockroach just because their mother treats them like one. You, as a lion, got those good grades, and got accepted to that university, and birthed those children, run the household, resolved that conflict, survived that struggle, climbed that mountain and scored that job.

So when 9 people tell you that you're smart, resilient, confident, beautiful, industrious, helpful, badass; believe the majority. You are one against 9. Join that club. Join the rest of the world that thinks your amazing and can do anything you set your heart to. What your mother has provoked you to believe about the world and yourself is over. It's done. You have disproved her time and time again. Listen to the people around you who are supportive and loving. Listen to people who are getting that great first impression. Listen to people who are happy to meet you. Listen to people who are enjoying getting to know you and are choosing to spend more time with you. Listen to people who enjoy the world and have done things you want to do. They are proof that the world is full of opportunity, not limits.

REWIRE YOUR BRAIN

Recap: Your emotionally abusive parent is on the side of treating you like you're not good enough. Stop being on her side. She is not the majority. It's evidence. Its logic. It's numbers.

1) Your first step should be to consider that you mother is wrong about who you are. All of you. Just - consider it. Roll that idea around. Meditate on it. Write it on a post it note (even if you currently think its a brazen lie) and put it somewhere that you can just look at it. You don't need to believe it yet. Just let it hang in the air around you, as though someone else has suggested it.
   a) My mom doesn't know me.
   b) How my mom describes me is not true.
   c) My mom's comments are subjective.
   d) What my mom says about who I am is bullshit.

2) Use the Bullshit Chart on thoughts about yourself (if you haven't already.) Particularly ones you know have come from your mother. Break it down into categories about yourself as a person:
   a) Your physical self image
   b) Your personality
   c) Your habits/behaviors
   d) Your achievements

3) Change definitive statements to neutral statements. This is a really basic tool of taking a statement about yourself or the world that you consider as true or a reality and putting it in the maybe or sometimes column.
   a) I'm impatient → I have felt and behaved both patiently and impatiently.
   b) I'm overly emotional → I have emotions.
   c) I'm not living up to my full potential → I have potential.
   d) I pick bad romantic partners → I've had both good and not so good romantic relationships.
   e) Other people find me too aggressive → some people dislike aggressive personalities
   f) No one is going to help, save, or comfort me → Some people are compassionate and helpful, some are not.
   g) People don't like 'blank' → everyone has different preferences.

4) Start asking around. A lot. Friends, family, strangers on a bus, post questions on your facebook feed or an online forum/group. Have conversations with everyone. Expand your access to the gigantic and infinite universe that is out there. The more you realize you don't know - the more fascinating life becomes. Variety is the spice of life. This proverb has been around for friggin ever. For a good reason. Accept that all viewpoints and experiences are real, valid, and true for the people who are expressing them.

5) Don't be afraid of sounding 'stupid.' Anyone who belittles you for asking a question is a giant asshole. They have their own issues they need to sort out. Trying to gain more knowledge is the most basic sign of intelligence.

6) Compare and decide what is right for you - or don't decide. Take all the viewpoints and conflicting information you're getting from others and hold them against one another. Or even let them blend and bleed into one another like a smeared rainbow. Work out what perspectives on the world are most helpful for you. It's not about being right - and it is not about being comfortable. You can believe something one day then collect new information tomorrow that makes your previous belief unbelievable. The point is to keep exploring for growth. What ideas make you feel strong? What perspectives help you feel confident? Why not choose those perspectives about yourself and life?

7) Wrap this chapter into Changing Your Internal & External Commentary. Almost all the tools in this book are meant to be used in conjunction with one another. Help yourself Take Control of your Internal Voice by experiencing all of the different options you have available. There is not one right way to talk to yourself or talk about the world. There are tons. There are also a ton of ways to 'not' talk to yourself and about the world. You'll run into both. Trust me. The point is to be aware of you options.

8) Realize that nothing is permanent. Not even tattoos are forever anymore. Even people who have lost both their legs can train on prosthetics and run marathons. Whoever you believe yourself to be, due to your mother's influence, can change. You do not have to remain the person you are. How you behave and the choices you make are not your personality, built in bricks and mortar. You can drop a bomb on your self image and rebuild. Or just remove the pieces you don't like and start gluing on things you find beautiful.

Next level: Both Kara Loewentheil and Dr. Joe Dispenza deliver the concept that our 'personalities' aren't actually real. Or at least - aren't set in stone. Introvert, extrovert, organized, Type A/B/C, creative, disciplined, wreckless - these are all things we can change. These are behaviors, actions, muscle memory, habits - and are not set in stone. Take a look at their work and concepts. You may find it extremely empowering to know that you can literally be anyone or anything you choose. You can just...change your mind.

Chapter 13

Rethink Forgiveness

Before I explain my views on forgiveness I think it's best to discuss my thoughts on anger and rage.

Anger and rage are both reactions rooted in fear. When we experience fear it means something is currently hurting us or we perceive it will hurt us in the near future. Whatever circumstance or person responsible becomes registered in our minds as a 'threat.' Anger and rage are the alarm bells in our head going "I don't like this! I'm scared!" We need these alarm bells of anger and rage to survive; to keep us safe.

Our minds & bodies have 3 reptilian responses to this: fight, flight or freeze.

- Fight is an active defence (or offense, actually) - shown through anger and rage.
- Flight is fear taking over - we run or hide, aka 'make an exit'
- Freeze is the response experienced when we are utterly unable to cope or register anything. We shut down, we are silent. There is no response.

What's interesting about Flight and Freeze is that even after our bodies & minds use these to respond in the moment, many of us still experience rage and anger 'about' whatever was threatening us, at a later time, after the situation is finished.

Example: Your mother makes an insulting or digging comment in front of other family members.

You choose to
    a) Make a digging comment back (fight/anger)
    b) Tell everyone your not feeling well and excuse yourself (flight/run or leave)
    c) Keep your lips sealed and let her carry on (freeze/shut down)

Despite flight and freeze not being an open display of anger, we often look back on these situations and feel anger or rage against our mothers for their hurtful behavior. Many of us carry these feelings with us for days, months, or years. This happens when it is repetitive and continuous, without repair. This doesn't happen in accidental circumstances. If it was an accidental situation, your mother would use empathy to realize what she said was hurtful, and she would apologize. She would also make an effort to not repeat similar comments in the future. This offers opportunity to repair and release of the offense.

Here is where we need to get very clear:

Repetitive and continuous harmful behaviour is abuse.
Our minds and bodies identify abuse as a threat.
When a person abuses us, they register in our minds as 'a threat.'
Our mind registers a threat when our boundaries are crossed.

Let's apply that to our relationship with our mothers:
When we get angry with our mothers for hurting us, our minds view her or her behavior as threatening because it has crossed boundaries we use to keep ourselves protected.

When our mothers are repeatedly emotionally abusive to us, we feel anger and rage. This anger and rage is our response to being threatened when she crosses our boundaries.

If you are still unclear about 'why' you are angry at your mother - please - broaden your scope of knowledge on this through as many other sources as possible. Be very confident in 'why' you are angry. I had my lack of understanding about this used against me for years.

My mother constantly used a really abusive tactic to defend herself and keep emotional control. She would ask "What have I ever done to hurt you?" I reacted by sharing a memory or situation. Only to have it turned around on me with one or more explanations:
1) I don't remember that happening
2) But that wasn't my intention, you misunderstood me
3) But you did 'such & such,' so I had to do those things

This is both narcissism and gaslighting. Instead of the healthy process of listening, responding with empathy & compassion then offering a form of repair - she used deflection and denial. She would discredit my memory and my feelings regarding the circumstance. Any time I would bring up a situation or memory as justification for my anger, her solution was to tell me my memory was incorrect, therefore my anger was unjustified.

Now we will talk about forgiveness.

Forgiveness in Western society is rampant with bullshit. Let us just lead with that. We are taught to forgive because it is the 'right thing to do.' We are taught that forgiveness will offer us peace of mind. We are taught that forgiving is a way for us to heal ourselves. I believe these reasons and goals of forgiveness taught to us are correct.

The problem with Western social norms around forgiveness is that we're taught that we 'should.' No matter the circumstances. Western ideas about forgiveness are deeply rooted in monotheistic, traditional western religions and biblical references; the most popular being 'turn the other cheek.' If you actually study these religions, God has an abundance of forgiveness. But we are human. To expect ourselves to be on par with God's ability to forgive is ridiculous. It is even stated that to participate in the process of forgiveness with God requires the 'desire to be forgiven.' It's a two way street. How can we be expected to forgive someone who does not wish to be forgiven, when even God himself will not (or cannot)? Regardless of the example set by religious dogmas; why are we socially pressured to forgive someone who does not participate in the request & acceptance process of this?

As the first part of the definition below explains, forgiveness is driven by an internal locus; our own change from within. Forgiveness is offered as the tool for us to let go and move on. But I don't think forgiveness should be a tool used by one person. Forgiveness should be a dual participant process. One must wish to be forgiven, in order for another to offer them forgiveness. When we give anything to another person - it is a meaningless process without their desire, acceptance or acknowledgement of what we are giving.

Let me offer you the Wikipedia definition of forgiveness to clear this up:
> **Forgiveness** *is the intentional and voluntary process by which a victim undergoes a change in feelings and attitude regarding an offense, lets go of negative emotions such as vengefulness, forswears recompense from or punishment of the offender, however legally or morally justified it might be, and with an increased ability to wish the offender well.*

Here is the important second part:
> *Forgiveness is different from condoning (failing to see the action as wrong and in need of forgiveness), excusing (not holding the offender as responsible for the action), forgetting (removing awareness of the offense from consciousness), pardoning (granted for an acknowledged offense by a representative of society, such as a judge), and reconciliation (restoration of a relationship).*

We are going to have to take this on, piece by piece.
1) *"The intentional and voluntary process by which a victim undergoes a change in feelings and attitude regarding an offense"*
   a) I support the changing of feelings and attitude about an offense. I also believe in letting go of negative emotions. These are both positive steps forward in helping or allowing our minds/hearts to heal
   b) The important word here is 'voluntary' - meaning suggestion or pressure from others to do so should have not value or weight in this decision

2) *"lets go of negative emotions such as vengefulness, forswears recompense from or punishment of the offender, however legally or morally justified it might be"*

    a) This part requires an extreme and powerful level of compassion. It is also the most necessary part of the process. This is the point where a person lets go of spending energy on their abuser. Any energy. You are not just letting go of the emotions; you are letting go of your wish for control of that person's behavior and future.

    b) This is also a form of finally accepting the age old saying "life isn't fair." Despite being told this repeatedly growing up, most of us pine for justice. Our entire social system is designed to deliver and execute justice. We know that life and the world don't offer karma in a way that is obvious enough for people to feel comfortable. If 'life' was actually fair, we would not need to design and implement systems of punishment or discipline, governed by people.

    To let go of our internal desire for our abuser(s) to be punished is the truest acceptance that we can exercise in regards to what we can and can't control. The only thing each of us has true control of is ourselves. That is the most powerful reality to live in.

3) *"with an increased ability to wish the offender well."*

    a) This. Is. Bullshit.

    b) If you are 'letting go' you should not be wishing your abuser anything. Nothing. You should not be thinking about them at all. You are not responsible nor should you be expected to take a road this high. This is a level of holiness that gets ridiculous.

    If you have been wronged by someone - they are not deserving of your positive energy - let alone any of your energy at all. Especially if that person has repeatedly wronged you, refuses to acknowledge any responsibility and does not offer genuine apologies. That person is not worthy of your time, energy or good will. Their existence should appear to be a hollow void in replacement of whatever space they are occupying. Harsh? Yes. Honest? Also yes.

4) *Forgiveness is different from condoning, excusing, forgetting, pardoning, and reconciliation*

    a) This is the part of the process that society continually screws up by leaving it out. Forgiving someone DOES NOT need be joined with the other actions listed directly above. Just because you've decided to forgive someone doesn't mean you need to (or should) let them back into your life. Showing compassion, understanding or empathy for someone's toxic behavior is not the same as opening up your boundaries for them to involve you in their toxic behavior moving forward.

b) True narcissists do not understand or want your forgiveness. They may request it, or even beg for it. But narcissists do not have the true capacity to believe they are ever wrong. They will treat your 'forgiveness' as condoning, excusing, forgetting, pardoning and reconciliation - especially if you LET THEM.

c) You are responsible for setting the terms and conditions of your forgiveness. You are responsible for communicating those terms and conditions, either verbally or through your actions and choices. You are responsible for defending your boundaries. You can only participate in one HALF of the forgiveness process. If your mother is a true narcissist, she is not, and will never be able to participate in the other half of 'accepting' your forgiveness - due to the belief that she doesn't need it. She will, on the other hand, treat your continued engagement with her as one of the other actions (condoning, excusing, forgetting, etc.)

The Forgiveness Anger Infinity Loop

This is where forgiveness and anger get mixed up. If you are still angry at your mother, you are not capable of truly participating in your half of forgiveness. Anger towards your mother means she is still registering as a threat to you. You must remove her from the threatening position she is holding in your life. This is what all of the tools in this book are for. It is time to rob her of the power to abuse you by developing healthy boundaries, self worth and your own set of standards for living a full and happy life. Forgiving her while recognizing that you are still angry with her - or even just reacting to her shitty behavior with anger - shows that her abusive, narcissistic nature still threatens you.

If you can exercise true forgiveness towards her but then participate in behavior that communicates condoning, excusing, forgetting, pardoning or reconciliation, she will continue (or at least try) to abuse you. Having healthy boundaries helps you stop at the tipping point. To exhale the anger is impressive. To have true feelings of forgiveness for her past behavior shows immense growth, self awareness, emotional strength and healing. Participating in a relationship dynamic where you continue to receive that abuse is not a required part of forgiveness.

When other people don't see or experience the abuse your mother doles out for you, they may suggest forgiveness as a tool; either for genuine intention of your healing, or selfish desire for more comfortable group dynamics that involve you, your mother and them. This is society's mistaken and ignorant good intentions. Forgiveness isn't a tool to solve a problem. Forgiveness is a process and activity - one which requires 2 or more people to participate. All the people involved in that process of forgiveness are using multiple life tools such as empathy, humility, compassion, ability to repair, and self awareness to participate. All those tools I just listed are not encompassed in a narcissist. Just remember that.

REWIRE YOUR BRAIN

Recap: You do not have to forgive your mother to move on. That is a lie made up by the proverbial 'they.' You can make 'moving on' look however the hell you want. Not being able to forgive your mother does not need to be a roadblock in your growth or change from Survivor to Thriver. There is no judge and jury, watching you with a check list. No one can stop you from deciding that you are going to move forward and grow as a person without forgiving your mother.

Yes - it's important to not waste energy blaming, it's important to let go of anger and resentment. Those things are good for you. What isn't good for you - is pretending to forgive someone, before you're ready.

1. Stop blaming. Recognize that your mother's damaged behavior didn't start with her. It's very possible that she can't help it. I know that sucks. Consider the idea that your mother may literally not have the capacity or capability to stop participating in her toxic behavior. She doesn't know how else to survive in this world. Her abuse is also her defence mechanism.

2. Participate in your half of the forgiveness. The tools in this book are all meant to diminish your mother's control over you, break her choke hold and vanquish her as a threat. As your self worth grows and you become a stronger person, her actions will feel less threatening to you, and you will have less rage. You need to voluntarily decide to let go of the negative emotions.

3. Stop at the edge. Do not pass go. Do not collect $200. Remember that forgetting, reconciling, condoning, excusing or pardoning your mother's behavior is not part of the deal. You do not have to do any of these things if you choose to forgive her. They are different. They are separate. It is also your responsibility to make that clear to anyone who seems confused about your voluntary choice to forgive.

4. Explore and gain confidence in your own ideas about forgiveness. Set up your own framework about what forgiveness looks like. What feels right for you? What works for you? It's ok to not be ready. It's also ok...to still be angry. Its ok to find forgiveness for a week - then have something trigger you and realize you're still mad. You're not perfect. 2 steps forward one step back is ok. 50 steps back is ok too. Just go back to the tools, find support, take a deep breath and start inching forward again. Its ok to fail. It's not ok to give up.

5.   Do not let your mother abuse new boundaries you've built. Forgiving her does not
      mean you have to be nice to her. It really doesn't. You can forgive her for past
      offenses. But if you verbalize boundaries that you have newly set to protect
      yourself - you do not need to offer her room to learn.
      a.   I don't like being talked to that way
      b.   Please don't share my private information with others
      c.   Please don't rearrange items in my home
      d.   Please keep your comments about my appearance to yourself
      e.   Please don't feed my kids out side of the meal times I've set when you care
           for them
      f.   Please don't call me during my work hours and expect me to respond

    If you have stated boundaries and she abuses/ignores them, you have every right
to communicate your anger and offer her relationship consequences for this. Do not forget
the 'consequence' part.

    In the next chapter we are going to get into these funny things called 'boundaries' I
keep talking about.

    You don't have enough of them.

Chapter 14
Extreme Boundaries

This chapter is about saying No.

Not just 'No' to your mother, but 'No' to everything and everyone who fucks with your boundaries. Even just a little. Even you.

This is also a chapter about personal accountability. Believe it or not, you fuck with your own boundaries. You break and abuse your own boundaries.

First - we need to understand what boundaries are, why people have them and how shitty yours are if you have an unloving/abusive/narcissistic parent. Having an emotionally abusive parent that repeatedly pushes or ignores your boundaries while growing up creates the behavioral habits of allowing everyone else to do it as well. It also trains you to not have respect for your own boundaries. Which is actually the same thing.

Allowing others to cross your boundaries, is actually 'you' not having respect for your own boundaries.

Developing boundaries was one of the biggest game changers I experienced during my process of recovery. It was shocking to realize how few I had and how bad I was at using the crippled ones that did exist. Being raised by a narcissist or abusive parent can leave you with little to no understanding of what boundaries are, why people should have them and what healthy ones look like. Changing this can affect so many areas of your life.

Why?
Because boundaries are directly related to your level of self worth.

Which means if we have poorly developed boundaries we are communicating to the entire world that we are ok with being treated poorly. What do you think that says about how we feel about our self as a person? Outlook not so good.

Not having well developed boundaries is what allows your mother (or anyone) to make you their continued abuse victim. This starts so early in life. We're taught repeatedly that trying to set or hold a boundary will get us punished, usually in the form of falling out of favor with our abuser. Falling out of favor with the person responsible for taking care of you can have very scary consequences when you're young. It can debilitate you with fear.

Developing boundaries is actually less of a tool and needs to be more of a living standard. But in order to get used to it, you need to practice. A lot. All the time. First with your mum and then with everyone else that is currently in your life and any new person that you allow into it.

A person's boundaries are what keep them emotionally (and physically) safe. You need them. Everyone does. If you are ever angry at someone, it's because they have crossed one of your boundaries. Most of those times, you've let them.

How to Begin

The first time I ever clearly communicated and <u>held</u> boundaries to my mother I was 25. I had set the following 3 boundaries:

1) I will not listen to her talk to me about my father being sick or talk to me about why and how he is sick.
2) She is not allowed to bring anything into my home and leave it there without my permission. Everything she brings in, she takes with her when she leaves.
3) The topic of our mother-daughter relationship is off limits unless a counselor is present.

More importantly, there were consequences for these boundaries which I communicated as well. For boundary 1 and 3, I would end the conversation. I would either walk away from her and be somewhere else, or I would change the subject, or I would hang up on her. It was that simple. For boundary 2, I would make sure the item was on, in or beside her bags by the door, ready to leave with her when she was ready to leave. Or it was going in the garbage. And I would remind her before she left that if she didn't take it, that's where it was going. In the garbage or to the thrift store, soon after her departure.

She lost her marbles over this.

My mother's response was to question why I was punishing her and labeled my requests 'repressive.' She wanted to pick fights with me about my boundaries. She used them as ammunition, questioning my emotional well-being, criticizing my treatment of her as my mother and attempting to shake my confidence behind their legitimacy.

Understanding the psychology behind this is frustrating. It is one of the first social rules we learn. When someone says "No thank you, I don't like that" or "Please don't" or "Stop" - you recognize that person is setting a boundary and (if you give a shit about them) you respect it as much as possible. But to have someone complain, harp on, and badger you about personal boundaries you've set is actually crazy.

Like - **bat shit**,

> **psycho**,

> # **loonie-tunes style,**

crazy.

That person is saying "I don't WANT TO treat you in a way that makes you feel respected."

The problem with being raised by someone who does that is: you think that's normal. It has been, all your life. One of the most difficult habits created by this abuse cycle is our training that setting boundaries comes with a punishment. That punishment comes in the form of losing someone's good favor. It's also usually followed by psychological attacks until you bend and submit.

Fast forward to a few years later when you have friends, or start your dating life. Then your professional life. How often do you feel you were talked into something you weren't comfortable with? How often did you make or have plans and they got derailed by someone else who wanted to be involved or wanted things just a bit more suited to them? How often do you excuse yourself from the responsibility of how a circumstance turned out for you, by blaming someone else who just kept pushing for their preferences? Or resent someone for behavior you said you don't like, but keep spending time with them anyway? Or look back on situations and feel like a piece of garbage...for not standing up for what you wanted?

I spent a bunch of time considering that the people I was allowing into my life were also abusive and toxic - that's not entirely true. In some cases, yes - that is true. As children raised in emotionally abusive relationships, we biologically flock to adult relationships that play out in a similar fashion because of familiarity.

What is more true - is that we often let regular people abuse our half-ass attempts at boundaries. Especially because we are scared of losing relationships and opportunities by saying no, and continuing to stand our ground.

Which is bullshit.

If it crosses your boundary - you shouldn't be participating. Furthermore: you should not be having relationships with people who want to cross your personal boundaries. You are the only person responsible for preventing this. There are tons of regular healthy people who will try to solve the problem of obtaining things in life that they want. There is nothing wrong with that. What goes wrong is the integrity of your boundary. If you make it clear that you are not offering something (time, permission, attention, space) they will find it...somewhere else.

It's even possible that completely healthy people in your life, which you feel are constantly hurting you or 'taking' from you - have no idea. Your ability to communicate your boundaries could be so corrupt that no one has any idea that you tried to set them in the first place.

Rewriting Boundaries

There are 2 ways to view this concept. Boundaries are actually a lot more complicated than people assume. There is a widely accepted definition of what boundaries are, as follows:

Boundaries:
The preferences we communicate, regarding how we wish to be treated.

The widely accepted view puts the responsibility in the hands of others. It's about them changing - for us. We share our preference, and if people don't treat us the way we've requested we become angry with them. We make our pain, hurt, discomfort their fault. When we have openly communicated a boundary and someone breaks it, we respond to them as though they've done something wrong.

Consider a rewording of this - which focuses on us being the responsible party for what is happening to us or around us.

Boundaries:
The circumstances in which we prefer to participate in, tolerate or accept.

We don't ever get to choose how someone else behaves. We can ask, request, insist, or demand. But each and every other person gets to choose their own behavior. So when you decide on a boundary, communicate that boundary and then someone chooses not to behave in a way that complies with your boundary, the next move - is up to you. People will just keep behaving how they want to behave. They can choose to change for you. But if they decide not to, it is your responsibility to change; your environment, your choices, your participation level.

So there are 2 problems created in regards to boundaries, when raised with dysfunctional parenting. One is realizing who is responsible for participating in our boundaries. We've just gone over that. It's you.

The second is a fear of the consequences when executing our boundaries. This is a huge lesson that can be really hard to learn and overcome. When we begin learning to drop the fear of punishment for holding ground on our boundaries, the rewards are slow to develop. The growing pains are very real.

Feeling lonely, feeling alone, and feeling isolated are all fucking hard. I have been there. Many times. Especially when I was young. It hurts so much. And I constantly compromised my self worth (my boundaries) to not feel any of those things.

At the beginning of this book I promised to not share frequent stories of pain and sadness from my past. I think so far I've done a pretty good job, focusing on stories that became positive learning points for me. So here are 3 more that turned out really well. The first - is actually the full tipping point for where I discovered this damage, explored and then starting repairing this damage. The second was while I was in the middle of this growth and building the skill. The third was an experience after I had gained a lot of strength in this skill and was able to flex it; then give no fucks over it bothering someone else.

Viva Las Vegas:

I started seeing a guy, long distance in the spring of 2018. We had met on a trip, through mutual friends. During a call, I was telling him about my cousin and I getting excited for our upcoming trip to Las Vegas in September.

"Awe! I love Vegas! The shows, the food, playing poker. That's going to be so great. Hey - what if I flew down and we could get some time together there?" He said.

"Oh! You'd do that? I'm not sure. I mean, that would be really cool, I'd love to see you. And we'd have a lot of fun in Vegas together."

"Oh yah! I could take you out for dinner and a show. The food there is amazing. Have you seen any of the performances?"

"Well I don't really do that when I go. My cousin and I do pool parties in the day and clubs at night. I don't really go for the food and shows - and I'm not sure. It's kind of a girl's trip..."

"What about just one night? How about that? Just one evening together. Trust me, I can fully entertain myself when I'm there the rest of the time. It would be so awesome to get just one evening together."

"Yah - I mean, that would be SO amazing. Dinner and a show sounds great. I've never done that before in Vegas. I kind of feel like that's ditching my cousin and our friend though. We're kind of a little unit while we're there. I'll talk to her about it. See if they would mind?"

In my head I'm like FUCK NO.
My trip, my vacation, my girls, my time.

But I couldn't bring myself to say those things. I liked this guy a lot and wanted to see him. I wanted to participate in the plans he was making for us, and I was worried about his feelings if I turned him down. If I hurt his feelings, or rejected him, or said no... would he take it that I don't want those things with him at all? What if this is the 'one' offer I get? If I say no this time, would he brush me off in return later? If I reject him, will he reject me back? I don't want that. Will he be mad, or upset? But even during the call - I was angry that he was asking for my time, during a trip that he wasn't involved in. Especially time away from my comrades that I was traveling with. But he was offering the date of a lifetime. The reason I don't do dinner and shows in Vegas is because I can't. I don't have the income for it. This might be an opportunity for me to have those experiences.

We had a second follow up call about it and some text messages. We talked about dates, what hotel he likes staying at, how close that is to the one we're booking, we flirted and joked over the future fantasy of us being in Vegas together. But as the idea solidified and he began asking for a confirmation on dates, and times... I was still avoiding a solid 'yes' and making feeble arguments and excuses against the plan.

I even complained to a friend about it. How mad I was. The more my long-distance beau pressed for confirmation, the more irritated I became with him. The anger developed with each excited and aloof step forward he made, while I felt more threatened and backed into a corner. He had no idea the trap he was wandering into.

Luckily, the friend I complained to was my personal Mr. Inquisitive 5000.
- Why don't you say no? What would happen if you did?
- Why does that bother you so much?
- Why do you let people do that to you?
- How come its so difficult for you to do that?
- Where do those perceptions come from?
- Why do you let other people infiltrate your plans?
- Why are you letting someone have your time and attention, just because they are asking for it, instead of choosing who you want to give it to?
- You get so mad when feel your time has been disrespected, why do you allow people to do that? If you place so much value on your time, why do you let just anybody have it when they ask?

These were such good questions. Ones I had never really explored with myself. My first step was to stop participating in the situation I was complaining about. By this point I had already become well versed in stopping the blame cycle, then adding my aggressive philosophies on top of everything I struggled with. If I had time to complain about something (especially out loud to someone else) then I had time to find a solution. Then apply that solution.

So I call him. I explain that I really want to see him again soon, but I felt like he invited himself along on a trip I had planned with my cousin and friend, and my time in Vegas was dedicated to being with them. Sorry - but if he's in Vegas at the same time as me, I won't have any time to offer him. I would prefer that him and I arrange our own trip together, that's just about him and I spending time together. Not split it with something else I already have planned.

And you know what? He was a totally great person about it. He said he completely understood. Nothing exploded (not during the conversation anyway.) He was very nice about it and said he was now looking forward to making plans for a trip that was just him and I. That, right there, was a very healthy, compassionate, and positive outcome and response. I deeply appreciated that.

After that phone conversation ended - I proceeded to melt into a self-destructive puddle. I ghosted my beau for a full month, putting him off and telling him I was really wrapped up in stuff at the moment. Or completely ignoring his calls and texts for days at a time. During which I was staring at my insides, strewn about, trying to find the dysfunctional bits of myself that might offer any understanding of why my boundaries were so shitty. I succumbed to another mini depression as I relived a vast expanse of memories pertaining to feeling goaded, walked on, coerced, and manipulated. Was it my fault? Or theirs? Did they make me? Or did I let them? Did I wrongfully demonize a ton of people? All my life, have I just been allowing people to take, take, take, from me - and placing the blame on everyone but myself?

Is the reason my life has felt so out of control, not because others have taken it from me, but simply because I have been afraid of keeping it for myself?

If I lower the quantity of what I allow inside my boundaries, will the quality of what is in my life increase?

More importantly, will that higher quality inflate to fill those vacant spaces I have previously labeled as feeling lonely, alone or rejected?

Why did I think that telling people 'no thank you' would equate loneliness?

After my short stint of living in my rear view mirror, I hopped into the driver's seat and ripped that cracked, narrow, piece of shit right off the windshield. I looked ahead, stomped on the gas and did some off road 4x4ing.

I had already applied this process to my mother. I had already cut her out; and held firm. I think by this time she had taken seriously my threats of a restraining order if she kept harassing me through phone calls, emails and texts. I wanted the space in my life, that my mother was taking up to be vacated. Setting boundaries, and rejecting her for noncompliance was cutting out the cancer. The space in my life I gained back didn't create loneliness; it created relief. The place she held was so diseased, it was easy to foresee the improved landscape. I had a greater trust in a positive outcome.

But it's not as easy to determine that in all of our relationships. I had put my foot down with my Dad & brother about their requests to reconsider my mother's banishment. But I wasn't as afraid of their abandonment. Their loving and supportive phone calls continued throughout the process.

Though my father actually spent quite a while not feeling comfortable with coming to see me after I cut out my mum. His fear of the (very real) emotional repercussions at home overpowered his desire to spend time with me, for a while. Especially if my mum found out he had spent time with my daughter, without her. He claimed that he "didn't feel like it was fair" to spend time with my daughter, without my mum getting to as well. He was committed to the idea that "seeing the grandchildren" was something him and my mum only did 'together.' Over time his own resentment and reasoning developed. He began making trips to spend time with just me, then started making trips to spend with both me and my daughter together. My mother's emotionally abusive behavior in the days leading up to his trips, and in the days after his returns now paled in comparison to his joy of seeing his daughter and granddaughter. He had also done an incredible amount of personal work in learning how to set his own boundaries, to limit the damage of her abuse.

The relationship between my brother and I saw almost no damage. His requests for me to suffer her ego and save everyone else from her temper tantrums were short lived. He began his own process of creating stronger boundaries, as my mother's growing abuse began to affect his wife. His focus on protecting the mother of his own children outweighed the comfort of protecting himself.

Downtown Ultrasound

In November of 2018 I experienced an Ovarian cyst rupture. It took 3 visits to my GP and a lot of complaining to get an ultrasound referral. It took 3 weeks for the only ultrasound clinic in my area to give me an appointment date (which you don't get to choose, they just give it to you) for a month and a half later. In total, I was receiving an ultrasound for an ovarian cyst rupture 3 months after the event. Meanwhile my recovery symptoms increased in their complexity and my GP turned me into a test subject to rule out all other gastro issues and dietary allergy possibilities. My GP explained that it was hard to confirm the rupture without the ultrasound, so there was no point in discussing options or treatments until that time.

I was becoming quite desperate. I had 3 options:
1. Continue waiting, while simply managing all of my random, anxiety provoking, uncomfortable, scary and painful recovery symptoms.

2. Take a full day off work and sit in emergency at the closest hospital, 40 minutes away, and wait anywhere between 3-6 hours until a doctor will hear my case. Now, to some people that might sound really easy. That was an immediate fix. But as a single mom, that's over $200 in lost take-home wages on my cheque. It's also the cost of gas there and back, and possibly not getting in to see a doctor, before I have to leave and get back into town to pick up my daughter from preschool. I had to weigh out the actual cost of that 'free' Canadian Health Care system (which isn't actually free.) Then since it wasn't an 'actual' emergency, I could pick which work day to take off; Wednesdays and Fridays being better choices than others. Which begs the question: if I can wait and plan, and still cost myself $200 plus gas and travel time; why bother at all?

3. My aunt had a plan. She knew this clinic in Vancouver that got people appointment times really quickly and they gave you appointment time options. She explained in detail how I could make this work:
   a. I was going to go see my doctor again. I was going to ask him to send a referral to that clinic for me. She was going to send me the address.
   b. The day after he sends it in, if they don't call me, I can call them. She was going to get me the number for the clinic.
   c. I could take a Friday off work and walk onto the ferry and bring my daughter with me. She would pick us up, drop me off at the clinic for my time, take my daughter to the park while I had my appointment, then pick me up after and drop us both back off at the ferry.

Great! So easy. I would still be taking a day off work, but I could get an appointment in about a week, I wouldn't have to worry about my daughter, no waiting in emerge for a full day. She would take care of all the driving, we could grab a coffee together, what a great day. That was REALLY nice of her to offer all of that. I had a problem and she had offered a solution.

But wait. Why am I taking a day off and going all the way to Vancouver for this? And why am I making another appointment with my doctor and asking him to send another referral? And why am I bringing my daughter with me on a day she's with her father usually (and has a full day of preschool)? And why am I using fuel to drive to the ferry, then paying for parking and then paying for the ferry ride (there and back)... She made it sound like such a great solution, but if you break down the details - not actually. She made it sound like all of that was so simple.

My aunt, bless her soul, loves to help people. She loves to save people. She also LOVES getting time with all of the new generation of little kids in the family. These things feed her. Which is fine. There is nothing wrong with that. The problem was: it was her plan. And this plan, put her in control; of my day, my time, my options and my experience.

This is one of many situations where my skills and tools for learning boundaries were flexed painfully. Like usual, I thanked her and said that sounded great. I got completely looped into the idea. But - after our conversation I did 3 things. I visualized what that day would look like with 'her' plan for me. Where my daughter would be, where I would have to spend money, at what time each part of my travel would happen, and after that plan had played out completely, what would I be looking back on at the end of my day.

Then I assessed each of those details. Was the result of having to participate in that worth my effort? I questioned how much I valued the result in comparison to the process it would take. Then, finally, I got a second opinion. I talked to someone else about my options and I had them help me compare it. I got an outside perspective from someone who had nothing to gain or lose in the situation. It took only a few minutes for someone else to be like "that sounds super stupid."

So I decided on my own plan. I called my aunt and thanked her for her offer again, but politely declined, letting her know I had made other arrangements. Then I executed the plan that worked best for me.

What I haven't mentioned yet - is how fucking hard this actually was. My aunt was offering to take care of me. I did not grow up with this. I have curled up against my fridge at 5 o'clock in the morning, moaning and complaining with as much stoicism as a 14 year old can while approaching appendicitis, begging my mother to take me to the hospital. Only for it to be calmly suggested, again, that I'm probably just hungry and should eat something. This was along with interjections of how long and unpleasant the wait in the emergency room often was; also what a waste of the medical systems resources it was to see a doctor over things that can be taken care of at home.

Having someone fawn over me while I am in either physical or emotional pain is a glorious privilege I was sternly denied while growing up.

So when someone says "I'll do that for you. I'll help you with that. Let me take care of all of those things. But - my way." I suspiciously raise my desperate gaze, waiting for the catch. Whether I can see it immediately or not, I weigh my desire to maintain control, against my pining and burning hunger to be 'taken care of.' Even the simple situation of having attention, versus being alone. I have repeatedly chosen toxic, pathetic, dysfunctional, gross and cheap attention over the prospect of being lonely.

Which leads me to my last story.

I'm Not Available
After I had spent quite a bit of time building and fortifying this skill, I was able to achieve checkmate in very few moves.

Me: Hey, I'm only available on Saturday this weekend. I have an event I'm attending on the mainland on Friday night. I won't be back until early afternoon on Saturday.

Them: Why the afternoon on Saturday? Is there anyway to see you earlier than that?

Me: I'm catching a late morning ferry and I don't feel like rushing in the morning. So I won't be back in town until early afternoon.

Them: Can I pay for you to take a flight back? So you're back in town earlier?

Me: Sure, that sounds really nice. I'll let you know which flight time when I figure it out.

Me later: Hey, I've actually decided not to go to the event on the mainland. I have some things at home that I'd really like to get done that are more important. No need to book a flight. But thank you for that offer.

Them: So you'll be in town Friday night? Can I see you?

Me: No, I'm sorry. I have a bunch of stuff that I really want to get done at home. That's why I cancelled attending the event. It's just too much in my schedule.

Them: I'd really like to see you. Why only Saturday? If you're not going to the mainland any more?

Me: I'm sorry, I said the reason I cancelled going to the event is because I had too much at home to do. I'll be happy to see you Saturday late morning.

Them: Julia, what's happening to our relationship? I thought things were going really well between us? I know you have a lot on your plate, but I don't understand why I can't see you on Friday night if you're in town. We barely get any time together. I know you said you have a really busy schedule, but things have been going really well, I think. What changed?

Me: There's nothing going wrong with our relationship! Everything is totally fine. I'm really, actually just not available on Friday. I'm really sorry.

Them:(their next message was similar to the previous one, and turned into some long argumentative bullshit...along with them telling me they didn't think I was being very 'fair.')

Me: I'm sorry, I'm no longer available on Saturday either.

Then I blocked their number. And never saw them again. I received one, very melodramatic email afterwards. Which I did not reply to - and that was it. I was extremely relieved that I found that GIANT reg flag as early as I did by setting boundaries and following through with consequences. Plus - now I had a free Saturday night!

After practice, practice, practice - setting boundaries and consequences became this ruthless game that delivered no end of pleasure. The results were becoming so delicious. Intoxicating.

The power made me feel like a true Goddess.

My choices.

My time.

My plans.

My happiness.

My values.

My worth.

I used to feel pressured into family situations and spending time with people that made me feel uncomfortable and resentful. I used to be so angry when guys would repeatedly request time that made my schedule too jam packed. Or when I felt I had 'wasted' my time on someone. I used to be so frustrated and disappointed when I would see people I was in relationships with getting what they wanted out of it, but I wasn't getting what I wanted.

When I began having and participating in healthy boundaries - my whole life changed. Before it was like constantly fighting in the dark, trying to navigate an ever shifting desert landscape. Clutching and grasping at the sand, not understanding why I couldn't hold on. Until I became the wind. I was now the gentle breeze that could tickle the leaves and enjoy their laughter, or a fierce storm, carving a path by uprooting trees I decided I didn't like having in my way.

Sounds amazing. But there is a gap. If you are addicted to avoiding feelings of loneliness, being alone, feeling isolated - this is a painful detox. If you fear people abandoning you for saying no to them - this is going to be fucking uncomfortable.

If you would rather spend time or share space with people or doing things you don't truly appreciate, rather than 'feel' or 'be' alone - you are going to experience some hard growing pains.

And those growing pains will be very worth it.

Your goal is to decide ahead of time what you value - before you participate. Then only participate in things you feel add value to your life. You will no longer be fearing the social or emotional repercussions of setting and holding boundaries. You will be utilizing your boundaries to communicate your high level of self respect and self worth. Which creates an environment for a higher quality of living.

REWIRE YOUR BRAIN

Creating boundaries after being raised by toxic parents has 2 components.

The first is learning who is truly responsible for respecting the boundaries you set. That person is ALWAYS you. You are the person who sets them, and executes them. You are also the person responsible for making changes when they are pushed against, on purpose or not.

The second is managing and eventually, banishing the fear and discomfort that comes with having & keeping your boundaries.

It's ok to spend some time saying 'No' to everything and everyone. It's ok to do a cleanse, and slowly add things back into your emotional nutrition plan to see what makes you feel good...and what doesn't. You can either clear all of the debris and start with a clear playing field, or locate your current boundaries, and slowly, methodically work on bringing them inwards.

Below are a list of activities and habits to practice. These will help with 2 things:
A) Help you make/find boundaries and then set or hold those boundaries for yourself, through establishing consequence
B) Form habits to change feelings of isolation/loneliness into opportunities for developing higher self worth. This is done by increasing the value you feel in where you offer your time and attention.

1. Set your schedule in advance. For the day, for your week and for your month. Don't just know where your time is going. Decide where you are putting it and spending it. Consciously.
    a. When will you be answering calls and messages from loved ones versus acquaintances?
    b. When will you be at work? At the gym? With your children? Doing self care? Doing chores? Having social time?
    c. More importantly: what, if anything, would you allow to 'interrupt' those scheduled activities?

2. When someone asks to be part of your schedule - decide if you want that as well (or if that is just something for them)?
    a. Are they suggesting something you already thought about asking for or arranging?
    b. Are you delighted at the opportunity? Or unsure of where you want to fit that in?
    c. Or are you already finding yourself agitated that you would have to move around important things in your schedule to participate?

3. If you feel like the cost vs gain ratio is more in their favor than makes you comfortable, think about what would make you feel like it's equal. In other words: mutual or symbiotic. Are you both going to offer each other what the other person/people are looking for in that circumstance?

4. Look past the moments of isolation. If someone is asking for your time, energy or attention - visualize how you think you will feel after participating.
   a. Does that situation feed you and your needs?
   b. Will you come out of that situation feelings drained? Or amazing and fulfilled?
   c. Only choose to participate in plans or situations that you feel enrich your life and self worth. You really shouldn't be participating in anything less than that.

5. If you are unsure - go into the situation with 2 things: no or low expectations and an exit strategy. If you met someone new and they've asked for a coffee date but it's both a bit of a squeeze in your schedule and you're not too sure if you like them - set boundaries for yourself and don't put all your eggs in one basket.
   Make a list of what you do and don't want to experience with a tipping point. If that person is bland, or doesn't have 'second date potential,' just leave. Your exit can be going to get in a workout you wanted. Or let a friend know you might need them and ask if it's ok for them to be on stand-by. Or have errands that you 'kind of have to run.' They don't need to be done if you enjoy the company of your coffee date companion, but if it doesn't work out - you now have extra time to do things you would find rewarding to get done.

6. When you feel lonely, alone or isolated and can feel yourself starting to approach bad choices about where to offer your time and attention - think about 3 things you wish you were doing most. Things that would make you feel like a really great person. Then figure out which one you could actually be doing right now. Go do that!

7. Call or message someone that you miss and wish you were spending time with to see if they're available. Even just for a 1-3 hour chat or facetime.

8. Send out 3 messages to tell people you love them, miss them and hope they're doing well. Don't indicate you need a reply. Just - send out the love and good energy.

9. When you need to communicate boundaries verbally - always communicate the consequence with it. It doesn't need to be a threat or punishment. It's not about the other person being 'bad.' It's not what you're going to do 'to them.' It's just what you are going to do, yourself. Leave, stop seeing them, hang up, not participate in social situations with them anymore, not drink with them, etc. Be clear, be consistent, don't back down.

Boundaries are a very important part of recovery; and recovery language. If other people in your life scoff at or react poorly to discussing boundaries, you should probably not be participating in a relationship with that person. Knowing who you ARE is only half the battle. The other half is knowing who you ARE NOT. Know what you will NOT tolerate, participate in, accept, or offer. That shows your character, which defines your integrity, which is where you find your self worth.

Chapter 15
Cutting Contact to Heal

"You can't heal in the same environment that made you sick"
- Erico Mesiano

Do not allow abuse to be the glue of your family. Growing up I watched my grandmother sink her teeth into her own children. She would make digs, pick their emotional scabs, make seemly aloof comments that had vicious, layered undertones. Some of her children did it back to her. Some of them did it to each other. It also rarely occurred between just 2 of them. Any overheard comment was an opening for someone else to join a side and take up arms. A shocking number of us in the family attended therapy and finally someone's therapist came up with the explanation that my grandmother and her children (my mother, her 3 sisters and brother) had an abuse style of 'eating their own young.'

Yet every Easter, Thanksgiving, Christmas, Birthdays...we still got together. We were told "that is what family does." Every once in a while there were fights or comments bad enough that someone didn't show up for a few gatherings. But with or without apologies being exchanged, enough other family members would goad the separatist to rejoin family functions and no one would talk about the incident that provoked their absence. There was no sharing, no repair.

When we continue to spend time or share space with people who treat us poorly it communicates that their bad behavior will be tolerated. When you refuse to share space or interact with someone because they treat you badly, you are setting an expectation for appropriate behavior and treatment of yourself and others. Someone being a member of your family does not excuse them from this expectation.

Someone being a family member should actually make this expectation more severe.

You need to ask yourself if you would continue having a relationship with the person your toxic mother 'is' if she wasn't your mother. If your mother did not share DNA with you, or didn't raise you - would you continue tolerating a relationship with her?

There is a very firm social regulation that we must revere our mothers. For everything they have done for us, all of their sacrifices, all of their love - we must appreciate, respect and honor them.

This. Is. Not. True.
This is - in fact - bullshit.

Does society hold the same expectations if a father is abusive?
Does society hold the same expectations if your mother physically abused you?

What gives emotionally abusive mothers this 'out?' Why do they have a 'get out of jail free' card?

We hear: "She means well. She just cares about you. She does it because she loves you. She's doing the best she can."

That's fine. That may also be very true. Your mother could actually care very deeply for you, and mean well. She most likely does love you. Despite the twisted and malicious ways she communicates that. But you are not required to accept that treatment in any relationship. No matter what someone has 'done for you.' That's one of the most misguided suggestions in society. That is some serious Stockholm bullshit, right there. Someone putting clothes on your back, a roof over your head and food on your plate does not give them the right to treat you poorly. Not ever.

A Legacy of Pain

Abusive, toxic mothers come from abusive, toxic experiences of their own. Basic. Every bully was a victim first. Tolerating, accepting and participating in an abusive or toxic relationship with your mother is creating the next touch-point in the legacy. You are collecting and absorbing the pain, fear and damage from her. And for years, you've been passing it out as well. You are reading this book and trying to collect these tools to recover from, undo and change the patterns you've developed from being emotionally abused. One of those tools is cutting off the infected area.

Look back and analyse the memories of abuse and how that pain bled out into the rest of your life. Any and every fight with your mother has touched someone else in your life. You sabotage a relationship with someone you were dating. You can't develop or keep solid, long term friendships. You get absolutely wasted and pick a fight with a stranger. You take out your insecurities on coworkers. You use unhealthy methods to pacify your uncomfortable internal turmoil. You stone wall and emotionally isolate yourself from your romantic partner. You withhold affection from your child in tough moments - or - you find yourself repeating your mother's exact parenting patterns.

Thought Experiment

Imagine someone has gifted you an ugly, poorly designed lamp. (Yes - this ugly dysfunctional lamp is a metaphor for your mother.) You don't like this lamp. It doesn't work well, no matter where in your house it's placed, it just feels in the way. It's an eyesore and a nunsense. But it was a gift. It feels rude to throw it out or give it away. You complain about it to everyone who will listen. You trip over the cord, sometimes it wont turn on even if you've changed the lightbulb, it has an odd buzzing noise sometimes and doesn't go with any of the other pleasant things in your home. Finally you get fed up and you put it in a closet; still unable to throw it out. But every time you open the closet you're reminded of how horrible it is. It's taking up space in your closet, that you need for other things. Then you have kids. They get old enough to pull it out of the closet, play with it and find it to be kind of a novelty. They don't experience all the layers and years of irritation with it that you do. But you're the one who has to deal with packing it back up at the end of that day and wrestling it back into the closet.

The years go by. The random moments you have to come into contact with that lamp just increase your resentment over your feeling that you have to hold on to it and keep it, even though it's such a hassle. Until finally one day - you decide to move, to upgrade your living situation. As you're packing the last pieces of your life that you want to take with you - you see the lamp. You look on it with pity and sadness. All the years of struggle, trying to find a place for it, trying to minimize it's negative presence in your life. Finally you ask "can't I just leave this behind?"

The answer is yes.

Every time you come into contact with your toxic, dysfunctional mother, you risk the potential of dragging out the legacy of pain, fear and abuse. Our goal is to stop the cycle. Our goal is to end that legacy. Our goal is to begin a new legacy beyond the reach of her damage - and ALL the damage she has collected from every previous contributor of that abuse legacy before her.

Epigenetics

You can actually change your DNA. Or rather - how your DNA operates and functions. It has now been proven that less than 5% of the diseases in the world are genetic. That means the other 95% can be avoided or prevented. Research has revealed that cardiovascular disease dragged through generations, cancer, obesity, and even trauma can be halted.

Another way of explaining this is to be predisposed, but not predetermined. Meaning: it's likely you will have similar health problems as your parents, but they are not inevitable. These health problems come from lifestyle choices and habits passed down through families. They are not fate or destiny.

If we change our environment and our lifestyle habits, in comparison to those of our genetically linked predecessors, we change which markers in our DNA become active and inactive.

The reason intergenerational abuse happens is because each new generation grows in a similar environment, as each set of parents pick up and act out the same abusive behavior as their own parents before them. It becomes written and encoded on to each set of children born into the legacy. The only way to change this is to change the environment and habits. When you become an adult and have the autonomy or perogative to choose your environment, then change your behavior and habits - you have the power to change how the legacy plays out. You can choose to have the abuse in your genetic make-up stop with you.

Only 5% of the diseases in the world are actually genetic. Abuse, toxic behavior & trauma are not genetically predetermined. They are a highly contagious sickness. But you can develop the antibodies.

The Mexican Standoff

My father and I would continually go through the back and forth of me arguing for him to leave his abuser, and he would argue for me to let mine back into my life. Our abuser was the same person - My Mother.

When I first started this process, things got worse. There were times when that light at the end of the tunnel would become completely devoured by the darkness. I have a huge family - and we have a lot of years and memories of shared space. So when I decided to cut my mother out, I had some very strong voices in opposition. Two of them being my brother and my dad. Her other top ranking victims.

They had 2 arguments; first, my choice to cut her out was hurting her. It was causing her depression, sadness, and pain. Denying her contact with me, as well as my child, her granddaughter, was uncompassionate, mean spirited and of course, immature. Second, this was causing her to lash out at others and if I would let her back into my life, or at least allow her access to my child, she would stop.

Both of these stories are fiction. They are lies. They are untruths. Furthermore, they are from the lips of people with the sole purpose of alleviating their own suffering. They are not advocating for my mother. They are advocating for themselves. Their goal is to lessen their own pain, by spreading out the load.

Abusive people have this bizarre delivery quota, as though they have a certain amount to dish out. If you chop off a piece of their punching bag, the remaining surface area starts getting punched more often. There is also something called 'narcissistic injury' where a narcissist experiences damage to their ego. Taking something from a narcissist they believe to have ownership of, threatens them psychologically and a reaffirmation of control must be established through dominant behavior.

So when I cut contact with my mother she became more abusive with the other people close to her. But not before she became more abusive towards me.

I cut physical & vocal contact first. I would not accept any arrangements to share space with her and I would not accept phone calls. So she emailed me. She texted me. They ranged from pathetic manipulation attempts to viciously cruel. They caused tears, confusion, madness, depression, guilt and shame, insecurity and fear.

She was finally silenced when I responded with an email explaining that anymore attempts to contact me would result in me seeking a police issued, no contact restraining order - and I copied a lawyer's office on the email. I also copied my therapist; and multiple family members. The silence was powerful. Day after day went by, and I heard nothing back. After a while, I was able to wake up and not worry. I eventually forgot to wake up and be worried at all.

But when my father began to visit again - there was always a section of our time together where he would ask me to reconsider. Every point he made, I would make a counterpoint. Then the next time he would visit, there would be a new argument from a new angle. This included the argument that my mother should be able to see my daughter, even if I didn't want to be present. I continued to refuse and became very angry with my dad. I felt that someone I loved was requesting that I return to a place of suffering. I felt I was being asked, by someone who says they love me, to walk over hot coals - to make the coals happy.

I have to hand it to my dad in the end - he put up a good fight. I'd never call him a quitter. I eventually set the boundary that I would no longer participate in discussions focused on him suggesting I let her back in my life or my daughters - alas he found other avenues.

Father's Day, June 2019
It started with the French Press. My mother had bought one and insisted on leaving it at my house 'for when she stayed over' (all 3 times a year.) I owned a coffee maker, as well as a single cup pour-over. But she preferred the French Press style. It would be nice for me to have in the house, why would she bring her own over and take it back with her each time? Or lord knows how excruciating it would be to go 1-3 mornings without her precious, French Press made coffee...FML.

After I had stopped allowing her to visit me, there was a collection of her items in my house; things I had borrowed, things she had gifted. I made the mistake of sending a shipment of these items back with my dad after one of his trips. So since he is respecting my boundaries of no longer trying to convince me to let my mother back into my life - He wants to explain that getting rid of all traces of her in my house, is also banishing traces of him. His argument was that since the French Press was purchased at a time when he and my mother shared their finances, that the French Press was half his. So not allowing it in my house was also getting rid of things that were his as well. I was easily able to counter his argument with a rapid-fire list of my mother's poor behaviour as a guest in my home, in comparison to his non-intrusive and respectful style.

Alas, the worst was yet to come. It was his lead in to explaining that we are all 50% of each of our parents. Which means we each house within us, each of our parents trauma, pain, and legacy of abuse. He has learned that he is 50% his mother's past trauma, and 50% his father's past trauma. More to the point - that I am 50% my mother - and I will never be rid of her. Not ever. Therefore my attempts to rid my home and my life of the physical objects which hold her essence, is all forenaught. I am stuck with her. Forever - regardless of my purging.

I turned on my father. I coiled my head and neck over my shoulder, and my body followed, like a giant serpent hearing the rustle of prey. I had done my research - I was nearly done writing this book. I had found strength and validity in my growth, my evolution and the new life I had created for myself. I would not tolerate defeatist, victim focused dogma.

I spoke slowly and calmly - mindful that my father still has to focus diligently to not fall into a freeze or dissociative state when sensing conflict and anger in someone.

I am more than the sum of my parts, I told him. I am learning to live beyond my damage. I will not be carrying that legacy of trauma and pain any further into this family line. I am breaking the cycle. People are comprised of their genetics, their experiences and their environment. I can alter my genetics, I can design my environment and I can choose my experiences. I will not be 50% of my mother. Then I told him to give himself some fucking credit for all of the work he has done to recover from his own past. To look at who he is now and how far he's come. How could he believe that garbage? How could he agree that he was entirely comprised of nothing more than the pain of his parents past? I told him whatever he was reading was trash and holding his thought patterns in an unhelpful, dark place.

Despite the rest of our visit being pleasant, full of good wine and our joy of cooking together, I was triggered. Despite my conviction and stoic delivery, I am not made of stone. He left in the afternoon of the next day and by 7pm I couldn't hold back tears. That evening, I lay on my kitchen floor at the foot of my stove, choking back nearly a full bottle of rosé and sobbing. Hard. I considered it. I questioned it. I actually explored "can I truly become a person beyond the abuse, pain, and trauma of my past? Or will I always carry it? Will I always and permanently carry my mother's pain and damage within me? Will she always be a part of me? No matter how hard I try to banish her from within?"

I called my best friend. I told her I need help. I told her exactly why I was crying. She said all the right things. She told me she loved me. She told me I did the right thing, to reach out and ask for support. She told me its ok to cry, that I'm not my mother and to drink all the wine I need to drink. I sat up. "Ok. I'm ok. I'm going to be ok." I said. Then we ended the call.

I got off the phone. I got off the floor.
Then I created the Trigger Recovery Checklist.

I slept hard. The next day, when people would ask, I admitted that I recently had a really hard moment, but that I was going to be ok. I didn't hide. I accepted hugs. I focused on healthy habits and keeping my normal schedule, despite my blotchy face and glossy eyeballs. I even got a couple laughs in over life being random and rolling with the punches.

And next time my dad came over, I told him what had happened after he left. We openly talked about it. We shared our thoughts and feelings that had grown and changed since his last visit. Our bond grew stronger. I also made him a promise, that I would stop trying to convince him to leave my mom. I realized it was just as stressful and painful. I apologized for all the times I had insisted that he hurry up and get out. We were both walking our own path, at our own pace - to cut her out.

Carving Your Own Path

Every persons' relationship with their mother is so unique. This is a fucking understatement. The process in which you choose to cut contact will be just as unique. So will how the events unfold to solidify this cut. I've read (probably) most of the ways to accomplish this. Hard copy letter, phone call, email, text, face to face, including a therapist, a family member, a friend, a law enforcement officer, a social worker, whatever. Then there is also setting her car on fire and standing on her lawn with **resting bitch face** until she comes running out of the house; then just raising an eyebrow with a good glare and walking away. Communication tools cover a colourful spectrum.

We don't need to go over the physical ways for you to tell your mum that she is no longer going to be a part of your life. The basic list is above. (I'm really sad I didn't pick the last one noted...) How you choose to do it - is not the point. Do what feels safe. Choose the method that feels most effective for your current relationship with your mum. Not rocket science.

What is most important: is that you know WHY you're doing it. Your 'why' will offer you more power than any restraining order, family support or charred property. Your conviction, integrity, self confidence, and grit in this situation will yield better results than any particular method you choose.

So if you skipped forward to this chapter without reading the rest of this book, here are some WHYs for cutting out your mum to heal from the abusive relationship between the 2 of you:

a) You don't participate in abusive relationships; with anyone
b) People who have a healthy level of self worth don't tolerate being treated poorly by others
c) You're not ok with being a victim
d) Your psychological health is important to you
e) You're not responsible for helping your mom become a better person
f) Nothing you do will change who your mom is
g) You're finished being part of an abusive family legacy
h) You don't have time to participate in painful relationships
i) The emotional and psychological health of your children is more important than tolerating your mother
j) Blood isn't thicker than peace of mind
k) YOU CANNOT HEAL IN THE ENVIRONMENT THAT MADE YOU SICK

Continuing a relationship with a toxic parent is like choosing to repeatedly visit Chernobyl or Fukushima. You will just keep absorbing all of that toxicity. Everytime you step off the area, you still have all of that radioactive garbage just dragging behind you and sloughing off on everything else you get near.

You NEED the space. In order to heal, to build immunity, to let antibodies develop - you need to find a place beyond. You need to learn to build an identity outside of your mother's existence. Healthy and secure bonding between parents and children has an entire component of support for a little human to develop independence. Autonomy. Abusive and toxic parenting does not support this growth. Continuing a relationship with that parent, even into adulthood, hinders, stunts and sabotages this growth.

You NEED the silence. There is no room in your head for your own voice, if her's is always in there. You should not be desperately trying to talk over her. Why would you fight to talk louder - when you can simply have her stop talking? You need the absence of her voice/words/ideas in order to create and hear your own clearly.

You may have the mother that doesn't give a shit. You say "Bye Felicia!" and she just stares at you like a stranger. You may have the mother that starts destroying cities and becomes the Fourth Reich, once again, on the hunt for lost artifacts whose possession they believe to be their birthright. Regardless of how it plays out, after you pull the plug and look around to see who noticed the interruption to regular programming, the purpose and reason behind your choice is what will determine your success.

It Does Not Have To Be Forever

When I started therapy specifically for recovery from a gaslighting narcissistic mother, I was asked what my goals were.

"I don't want her words and behavior to have the effect on me that they do. I don't want her to have so much power over my reactions."

My family is big, and close. We try to get together and meet frequently throughout the year. We are also in the season of weddings and new babies with my cousins and siblings. Staying away, simply because my mother is attending is not ok with me. I didn't want to have her existence control my whereabouts or access to family gatherings. I felt that simply cutting her out of my life (as peaceful and simple as that looked) was a cop out. To simply avoid her, wasn't going to do anything helpful.

What I wanted was to not have her words trigger anything. I wanted her digs - to just not be digs to me. I wanted the toxic layers and history behind her comments to not exist. I wanted the fact that she was my mom, and horrible at loving me - to just not matter. I wanted the pain to go away. I wanted to be stronger than the trauma. I didn't want to be a victim of her damage. Whether she was present or not. No matter what she chose to do. I wanted my feelings, thoughts, responses, to not be constantly warped by all the shitty things she does.

I wanted to change. I already knew from a few trial and error runs, that she wasn't going to. If she wasn't going to get better, and our relationship wasn't going to get better, the last thing left was me.

I think in total I was absent from family gatherings for 14 months. I missed 2 Easters, 2 Thanksgivings, a Christmas and a baby shower, plus numerous birthday gatherings. It sucks and it's hard to understand that she was the toxic element, but I was the one who had to excommunicate myself. Actually, it's aggravating as all hell. But the power gained is worth it. The amount I was able to achieve by being away from her astonishes myself, my therapist and my close friends & family who have watched my journey. I am not the same person I was, when I started this journey. Not at all.

I needed to silence her voice to find my own. I needed repeated experiences in repair, healthy relationships, and positive reinforcement to solidify those lifestyle habits. I also needed them to be uninterrupted by her. I needed to not have a wolf at the edge of my support circle, waiting for a break in the crowd. The absence of the toxic relationship with my mother made room for me to build such a strong relationship with the person that I want to be. That foundation is so solid now. Those bricks and mortar are so tight. I created an environment for myself where I could be safely vulnerable. This allowed me to learn, explore, grow, fall, make mistakes, and find massive potential without a constant undertone or anticipation of fear, pain and rage.

That is the most significant difference between trying to grow while remaining connected to an abuser vs. cutting them out. Learning while in a stage of fear or pain creates conditions for poor quality wiring. You need to design an optimal growth environment for yourself. If you want to heal, you need to surround yourself with healthy and supportive people & circumstances. Which means you need to sever ties with people and circumstances that create a suboptimal growth environment.

When you feel strong in that growth, when you feel confident in who you are, your self respect and self worth - toxic people don't really exist anymore.

REWIRE YOUR LIFE

1. Know WHY you are choosing to cut your mother out of your life. Be sure that is the reason. Choose a back up reason. Make a fucking 6 point list. Focus on one - or make the list endless. Whatever makes you SURE this is what you need to do. Do you want to prevent the same parenting patterns? Do you want your children to have a better relationship with their parents than you did? Do you want to stop having anxiety and depression problems? Do you want to stop having fucked up romantic relationships? Do you want to access your true career potential through recognizing your self worth? Do you want to stop feeling tortured by the one person who is supposed to show you unconditional love? Do you want to break the cycle of trauma and abuse in your family?

2. Make goals for cutting out your mother. How are YOU going to change? Who are YOU going to be? How do you want your life to change? What are you going to be doing differently? It's ok to start with who you are NOT going to be any more. It's a significant half of the battle.

3. When you request no-contact, have consequences for noncompliance. FOLLOW THROUGH. Don't be a wuss. Use statements, be clear, do not leave openings for counter arguments. Ask for help in writing or practicing what you will say. Create a script. Remember: it's not a discussion. You are communicating information. It's not up for debate. You are not looking for a rebuttal.

4. If things get ugly, keep documentation. Keep text messages, emails, voicemails, all of it. Request that your therapist help you go over drafts of written contact you plan to have with your mother. Also request their support in handling your own reactions to any of your mother's responses. Request a law firm keep records. Know what qualifies as harassment in your province, state, district. (Some officers consider 3 attempts at contact after 1 request to stop is considered harassment and qualifies for gaining a no-contact restraining order.)

5. When you are not using these documents or records - put them away. Do not reread them a million times. Do not get caught in the loop of micro-analyzing every last word and tone. Let it go. Put it away. Go live your new, mother-free life. Unbothered.

6. Some of your friends and family will not understand. That's ok. It's you who needs to make peace with that. Some people who question or argue with you can't understand. They don't have the capacity. No amount of explaining will help them. It's beyond their depths. Some people don't want to understand. It threatens their framework of reality. It makes them uncomfortable. Again - you need to make peace with that. It's not your job to help them see the light. If someone is asking politely or inquisitively, feel free to engage. Otherwise you're just wasting your breath. If you want to keep certain individuals in your life, avoid the subject, set discussion boundaries. By this point in the book - you should know how to deal with this.

7. Some of your friends and family will understand. I had multiple friends and family respond with "Oh, that makes sense, your mom is fucking crazy." Or even "Good for you!" Connect with these people in creating your 'Majority.' Ask if they would be willing to share any memories with you that would help you gain insight or validation of your experiences. It can sometimes shed light on how other people identify 'red flag' behavior. Also explore their potential to be your support network. Those who are open to the concept of cutting out toxic or abusive people, especially a mother, are people who usually just have love to give, no matter your complicated choices.

8. Besides having to stay strong in the face of others who are questioning your choice - you will need to stay strong when you question yourself. It will happen. Set yourself up for success. Ask a friend to be your play back button. Everytime you reconsider your choices, go to that friends and ask THEM to remind you why you did this. Or make sure that list of WHYs is somewhere in hard copy, easy to find and written in big bold letters. Some of us will waiver in the face of harassment. Some of us will waiver in the tepid silence. Regardless of how this plays out for you - you will question your choice to cut your mother out. Even if you've decided it's not permanent. Make a plan for these moments ahead of time and ask for help and support with this plan.

9. If/when you decide to share space with your mother again - don't do it alone. Don't do it until you're sure you're ready. I made plans for 2 family gatherings and pulled out last minute, before finally attending one. You're allowed to change your mind. You're allowed to say you might see her, then choose to never see her. Or start with 'never' and move to maybe. It's always up to you. Always.

Recap to Rewire

A typical conclusion for a self help book would have that one last passionate call to action. It takes that last chance - while the author still has your attention - to convince you that everything in this book will change your life. That you NEED to believe them and the concepts which have been expressed therein.

We're not going to do that. You'll change your life if you feel like it. I haven't presented you with any shocking concepts that have never been offered before. What we are going to do is review the tools. Then we will review the top tips and reminders on ways to apply each of those tools. It's the cheat sheet on changing your current habits and breaking the toxic cycle you were raised into.

Because that is what I would find most helpful.

Tool 1: Know Thy Self
Overview: This book is for women who are tired of failing at life with all of the 'middle road' attempts to recover from having a shitty mother. You have insight and understanding as to 'why' you have cyclical depression, low self worth and a perceptual tendency to self sabotage your own life & relationships. Up until this point, nothing you have tried seems to be getting you past the feeling that you're simply surviving. Now you're seriously fed up. Now you're ready to Thrive, instead of just Survive.

Rewire: Use the tools offered in this book repeatedly to start building the foundation of coping mechanisms for life. Habits and skills which you were not offered because your main caregiver didn't know how to love you in a healthy way. Study these tools and carry them with you at all times. When you start struggling with anything in your life - pull one out; see if it fits. If yes, great. If not, pull out another tool and try that one. Keep trying. You can handle this.

Tool 2: Fluid Acceptance
Overview: You will never be done healing. You will never be done the journey for recovery - because life keeps 'happening.' Perpetually. 'Life' is constant. Throw the idea of becoming perfect or a 'finished project' out the fucking window. On the flipside - do not sink into the idea that you will be forever broken. Live in the middle. That grey zone offers way more room, and is WAY more comfortable than the satisfaction of having a hard lined label of who you are.

Rewire: This one takes constant practice. It needs to be a habit you develop and ingrain into your brain. Compare and despair; no one is perfect - that means you too. Stop using 'perfect' as an empirical measurement. It is not helpful. Throw the word perfect out the fucking window. Find and use matras for when you make mistakes. Ones that help you calm down, self soothe and focus on finding a solution or repairing. Live in the grey zone and make it your bitch. Remember: Sometimes, maybe, kind of!

Tool 3: Get Aggressive

Overview: You have to NEED this. Being a victim creates a lot of anger and rage. That's a lot of negative and wasted energy. But you can't just 'release it' in hopes of healing. Energy doesn't work that way. But you can craft it to change your course. Start using that energy in a passionate and productive way for yourself. Your current aggressive, assertive, driven, hardcore, badass self can find a higher purpose.

Rewire: Get serious about not carrying on the cycle of intergenerational abuse between mothers and daughters. Make it a service you provide to the community of people you love. How? Start crafting yourself into the healthy, loving, open, genuinely powerful person you could be - despite your damaged upbringing. Set goals on bettering yourself. Commit to breaking habits, know who you don't want to be and decide who you're going to be from now on. Stop fucking around when it comes to your recovery. Stop pushing it aside for everything else in your life. Because guess what - everything else gets easier when you start living beyond your damage.

Tool 4: Absorb Growth Style Knowledge

Overview: Stop obsessing about and absorbing information that tells you how and why you are damaged. This information holds you in the mindset of the person you used to be and the person you are now. You're trying to change that - which means you need to change the information in your environment. You need to start accessing information that focuses your thought patterns on who you want to become.

Rewire: Growth style media offers healthy support and positive guidance in the confines of your personal & private safezone. Jump on the bandwagon. Choose literature, videos, podcasts or any source of knowledge that is encouraging, enlightening, supportive, positive and progressive. Create a schedule or game for yourself to start making time to bring this into your life. Your phone is literally a portable supercomputer. You have no excuse.

Tool 5: Own Your Internal Voice

Overview: Our internal dialogue is almost always the voice of the main caregiver we had growing up. In the case of unloved daughters - its our mother's toxic dialogue. This is how the implicit and explicit messages she offered you about life got stuck in there while growing up. This goes for how we speak to ourselves, as well as how we internally comment on the world around us. This is why, even when she's not around, we shame, degrade, discourage and sabotage ourselves constantly. Stop that.

Rewire: We need to get rid of the current voice or dialogue style in our head and replace it with a healthy, loving, supportive, accepting, compassionate and tolerant one. Set up triggers and reminders when your mother's negative commentary shows up within you. Create mantras to replace the shitty phrases and words you currently use. Imagine you are talking to a child or your own child in the most loving way possible. Turn that inward. Also, when you find yourself commenting negatively on the world around you, focus on asking questions and having an attitude of curiosity or wonder vs. judgement. Remember that anger and abuse to yourself and others comes from fear and pain. Changing your internal climate will change how you experience the world outside of yourself.

Tool 6: Stop Blaming

Overview: Who you are is YOUR responsibility, and no one else's. How you became that way may, or may not be, the result of the actions of someone else. Placing fault or blame are not helpful and are not a productive use of your energy. You need to stop it immediately. The amount of time we waste on blaming our mothers for who we are and blaming other people, or our circumstances, for how our life is going is fucking useless. It changes nothing. Stop talking about it. Put that shit down. Let go of the baggage. All of that energy could be serving the purpose of you getting better sleep, being a better parent, a better partner, bossing your career, and lowering your cortisol (the stress hormone that keeps people fat.)

Rewire: Find other pathways and options for your mind when you get sucked into the thought cycles of blame. Having past memories about your mum that make you angry? Find mantras for your present. Becoming stressed and anxious about future confrontations with your toxic parent? Create mantras that focus on your self control and accepting your lack of control of others' choices and actions. Complaining about your shitty parent to someone else? Close the conversation on it for them and yourself with "And that is a topic I'm not talking about anymore because its a waste of my time and energy." Acknowledge the extra space and time in your life no longer taken up by blame and finger pointing. Then go put it somewhere fucking useful.

Tool 7: Trade Your Addictions for Accomplishments

Overview: Being raised by abusive or toxic parents designs us with low self worth. We become addicted to doing things that make us feel 'good' or 'better' to self soothe our feelings of despair and inadequacy. This never corrects the feelings of low self worth. It just keeps us on the never ending chase to find relief from our internal turmoil. We need to change our focus to participating in situations and doing things that make us feel competent & capable. This is what grows self worth, self respect, self love and self discipline.

Rewire: Start by making your goals so fucking easy its hard to screw it up. Spend an hour researching a dream, instead of watching tv. Sign up for a group class with a friend that won't let you skip out, before you crush a bottle of wine together. Start pressing the snooze button on your current addictions. Put cleaning, shopping, drinking, or promiscuity on the other side of a task that builds towards a goal or dream you've been putting off. Consider a journal where you fill in or check off each mini step you take towards being successful in your goal.

Tool 8: Get Vulnerable

Overview: Vulnerability is the new black. Get on board. The rest of the world will not punish your vulnerabilities the same way your shitty mother did (or does.) We need to let go of the constant feelings of inadequacy, lack of control, incapability and presumed inevitable failure. We need to get honest with ourselves and other people when it comes to these feelings. Especially because they are common, normal and necessary as a human. Then we need to learn how to ask for, and accept, help.

Change your beliefs around flaws and damage. You are not hopelessly flawed or permanently broken. You have areas under development. Those are the parts of you that others will connect with. The parts of you that are in evolution are where bonds are forged. Then level up and learn how to have positive and powerful feelings about your vulnerability.

Rewire: Make your vulnerabilities your gateway. Stop isolating yourself and hiding. Go find other beginners and rookies. Let them set an example of how to laugh at yourself and make the learning curve the ride of your life. Use the tools in changing your internal voice to reconstruct your dialogue regarding your vulnerabilities. Stop lying to yourself and others about being ok. You don't need to. Ever. Then split your vulnerabilities in half. Decide which ones to work on and which ones you're going to keep so you can flash them around like a peacock in heat. Identify your positive experiences when you get through expressing a vulnerability and find ways to repeat it and level up. Last but not least, commit to setting a good example for others. Make it not about you. Make it about showing others who are struggling, how incredible it can be to live a colourful life without any fucking fear.

Tool 9: Learn to Repair

Overview: Being raised in an abusive relationship robs a child of learning to repair in conflicts with others, as well as one's self. Repairing is already a challenge for the average person - and it's that much harder for those of us dealing with past abuse & trauma. We need this skill in order to develop integrity, strength of character and build deeper bonds with people around us. This in turn heightens our feelings of positive self worth. Repairing is about respecting other peoples' boundaries, your own boundaries and communicating compassion & empathy - towards others and yourself. We need to stop burning bridges and stop fueling the fire of shame and fear.

Rewire: Breaking down the process of repair into baby steps really helps with learning this skill. Repairing with yourself versus other people looks a little different. When repairing with others, it's never too late, don't take on more than your half, set your own comfort levels, know that you can change your mind, know 'why' you're doing it and accept that you can't control the actions of the other person involved. When repairing with yourself - be relentless. Do it immediately, push your comfort zones, find your limits and work on repairing with yourself until your so zen that Buddha would offer you a high-five.

Identify what abusive people do to victimize others in a repair situation. Stand your ground. Don't take on more than your half.

Tool 10: Force Transformation from Insight

Overview: Gaining insight is necessary - but it must be put to work. Knowledge is not power; it's potential power. Unless we 'do something' with the understanding we have developed within ourselves, you're ignoring it's value and purpose. It's important to spend time exploring who you are and how you work. When you figure out the pieces that aren't working, you need to repair them, replace them or throw out the whole system and start building anew. It takes a lot of effort and time to change who you are and how you behave. So you better fuel up and get started. Your other option is continuing to feel like shit about yourself and your life.

Rewire: When you do insight work and dig into the 'why' of who you are and how you function, don't focus on blame. Focus on responsibility. This is how you operate. If you don't like it - YOU have to change it. Outline your solutions that you're going to apply to those squeaky wheels. Surround yourself and build an environment that has reminders of your new concepts, ideas and direction in life. Every problem area you uncover needs a construction plan. Give it a name and decide what you're going to do about it. As you explore solutions, don't be afraid to change gears, pick a new path or shock yourself. You don't have to be 'right' but you need to keep expanding your mind and pushing growth. No one else is going to do it for you.

Don't forget: 70% on who you are going to be right now, 20% on who you're going to be tomorrow, 10% on who you were.

Tool 11: Trust in the Majority

Overview: Toxic parenting, especially when it involves gaslighting, can really warp our reality. Both the world around us, and the world within us can become largely contoured but the subjective messages we are fed by an abusive parent. As children, we are dangerously susceptible to filling in the gaps in order to make sense of ourselves and our world to survive. Now that we are adults, we need to challenge these beliefs so that we can stop being hindered by this framework. These ideas have trapped us. You can't live in a world you don't know, or have been told, doesn't exist. Our goal is to begin expanding our understanding of the other realities that are possible for us. There is potential for us to be the person we were taught it was impossible to be. Shedding the lies you have been fed breaks the limitations you repeatedly run into. Your health, your romantic life, your relationships, your career, your parenting, your mental stability, and your self worth can all reach new levels by getting a better handle on the reality beyond your damaged upbringing.

Rewire: Start toying with the idea that your mother or toxic parent is wrong about who YOU are. Just you. Whatever they have told you, however they have labeled you - just consider that it is wrong.

Take behaviors, habits and personality traits you believe yourself to have and take away definitive statements. Practice explaining yourself as a 'sometimes' person.

Next, start asking other people to confirm or deny those descriptions of you. Find people who you can pressure into giving you honest feedback. Don't be afraid to sound stupid. Anyone who makes you feel dumb for asking questions is an asshole.

Then start making choices. After collecting a broader perspective on 'who you really are' start choosing what ideas can stay, and what can go. It's not about being 'right.' It sure as fuck isn't about being comfortable. But start choosing a perspective of your life that is helpful - one where you see room for growth. Apply your more realistic view of yourself to the tool of changing your internal voice. Remember nothing is permanent. Who you are is not who you are going to be forever. It shouldn't be. That's lazy and gross.

Then go find Kara Loewentheil and let her explain why you don't actually even have a personality.

Tool 12: Rethink Forgiveness

Overview: Before you can approach forgiveness, one must understand anger and fear. Feeling threatened or in danger sets off survival alarm bells, often developing into this anger. Our brains create negative emotions associated with things that threaten us - such as toxic/abusive caretakers. While that emotionally negative connection is still present it very difficult to voluntarily *"undergo a change in feelings and attitude regarding an offense."* Western society puts stupid amounts of pressure on people to forgive; and for the wrong reasons. Forgiveness is not a tool for healing from an offense, it's a duel participant process. You can only participate in your half; and it's not going to look perfect. If your mother is a narcissist, she does not embody the social tools to participate in this. If you are still angry with your mother, she is still registering as a threat. Condoning, excusing, pardoning and reconciliation are not part of forgiveness. They are just other ways of allowing offenses to continue.

You're also allowed to not forgive. Having someone register as a threat is part of your survival instincts.

Rewire: It's important for you to understand that forgiveness is not the gatekeeper to your healing and growth. You don't 'have to' forgive your mother in order to move forward with your life and start thriving. It's more important for you to let go of blame and resentment - those are big time wasters. So is pretending to forgive someone. Especially when you haven't decided what your forgiveness looks like.

Stop blaming, only participate in your half, and don't mix up forgiveness with other bullshit like excusing, condoning, or reconciliation. It's also ok to forgive for a bit, get angry again, and learn your half all over again. Set new boundaries, offer new consequences, and don't expect an apology. Forgiveness isn't a box you have to check to become a better person. Society doesn't get to define yours. It's <u>voluntary.</u>

Tool 13: Extreme Boundaries

Overview: Setting boundaries in the hopes that people will respect them and treat us a certain way is lazy. Your boundaries are about what you are willing to participate in. If you are constantly feeling walked on, pushed around or coerced into circumstances - that's your lack of communication or lack of consequence. Neither of which need to be threats or punishments. Setting and keeping boundaries is a lifestyle habit required to establish your self worth and self respect. It communicates to others how much you value yourself. When you treat yourself well, people who don't - will stop showing up. Exercising healthy boundaries will also attract other people into your life that have them too. Although extremely tough to learn, saying 'no' to people does not isolate you. It opens up your life to <u>higher quality</u> relationships and forces you to consider the higher <u>value</u> of your time and attention. We need to disconnect the wires that tell us setting boundaries will get us punished and cause our loved ones to recoil from us.

Rewire: It's time to get cut throat. Take responsibility for enforcing your boundaries; with others and with yourself. Make your schedules and predetermine where you are going to put your time and energy, every hour of every day. Also decide what and who is either worthy or not worthy of interrupting what you already have planned. Most of all - go into your chosen circumstances with what you would like to get out of that time and shared experience. Communicate, reiterate, and follow through.

When saying 'no' to someone causes feelings of isolation or loneliness, develop routines to self soothe with healthy replacements. Stop waiting for people and opportunities to come to you. Actively choose what and with who you would like to be spending your time. Start with 'best case scenario' and go from there. Treat your time and energy as your most valuable asset. Anyone else who doesn't shouldn't be allowed to have it.

Tool 14: Stop the Cycle of Abuse

Overview: You cannot heal in the environment that made you sick. Cut off the infected area. There is absolutely no logical or acceptable reason to stay in a relationship with someone abusive. Not ever. Continuing to participate in a toxic relationship with a parent is dragging out a legacy of intergenerational abuse. Look into epigenetics and learn about why that doesn't need to happen and that you can change almost anything you believe to be unavoidable in your family tree. Search hard for your reason to live beyond this damage. Make it about more than just yourself - though that should be reason enough. Get space, get time, find silence, find your own voice amongst it, then grow and flourish into the yawning void her absence has created.

Then know - that once you have moved past identifying as a victim or survivor, you now have the tools to forever guard yourself and recover if necessary.

Rewire: Knowing WHY you're cutting out an abusive parent should light you up like a fireworks barge. This is your greatest weapon. Set your goals, and get a failsafe network. Use firm language, this isn't a discussion. Document your contact, and put it away when not in use (so you don't obsess over it.) Some people will understand and some will not. Don't concern yourself with nay-sayers. Identify your support network. Then when, or if ever, you're strong enough to share space again - don't do it alone. There is no reason to offer your valuable time and energy on someone who doesn't show you respect, love, kindness and compassion.

It's time to start living beyond your damage. Be greater than the sum of your parts. Stop just 'surviving' this life and start thriving in this life. You're not broken, you were just missing some tools. Don't blame your toxic parent - they didn't have them either. This is your responsibility. Make it your goal to stop the legacy of pain, abuse and trauma you are caught in. You have the tools to do this. Now breath deep - and go crush this.

This book isn't going to change your life.

You are.

<u>Trigger Recovery Checklist</u>

In June 2019 I was triggered during a visit with my dad, during Father's Day weekend. He arrived on a Saturday about 11am and left the next day around 2pm. During the course of his stay - the majority of our conversations revolved around my mother, trauma, pain, anger, our family's legacy and cycle of abuse and, of course, his newest arguments against my choice to excommunicate her. By 8:45pm on Sunday I was laying on my cold, laminate floor in front of my stove. My head was on my floppy, faux leather purse, being soaked with my tears while my fingers were wrapped around the last bottle of wine in my house. I sobbed quietly - so my daughter wouldn't hear me. I cringed and my chin would tuck into my chest, ribs curling in like a child's over excited fingers clenching a breathless teddy. My brows furrowed to the point of pain and my eyes shut so tight I was gaining my first set of crows feet.

I texted my best friend. I reached out. She called. All I can remember of that phone call are my words "I'm so angry at (my ex husband.) I'm so angry at (my current partner.) I'm so angry at my mum. I'm - SO ANGRY." I said this through tears, and sobs. I remember choking on these words. But as I calmed down, I remember her asking "what can I say that will help you right now." I told her "Tell me about your day. Tell me you had a good day."

It is so important for us to remember that 50 steps back is not failure. This is the entire point of the book.

You. Have. Tools. Now.

Triggers happen. They are real. They are valid. There is nothing wrong with you. It is ok to fall. It is not ok to give up. Remember that you are not broken. This is a set back. Fluid Acceptance. This happens. It's normal. You can handle this. Take a moment. Shut down, shut off, check out. Rest.

Then make your plan.

When you get triggered:

1) **Do Not Isolate.**
2) Be honest, genuine and raw about your pain - to yourself & others
3) Limit drinking, over eating, over exercising, obsessive cleaning or any other destructive self soothing habits
4) Take 'thought breaks' & rest your emotional mind (colouring, knitting, puzzles, etc)
5) Find growth style support
6) Find someone who will help you do an incident debrief
7) Make yourself sleep
8) Talk to yourself in a way you appreciate.
9) Make 30% of your thoughts insight - 70% transformation.
10) Live beyond your damage. You are not your past trauma.
11) **Do Not Isolate.**
12) **Do Not Isolate.**
13) **Do Not Isolate.**

Write these down. Write these out. Put them on your wall. On your bathroom mirror. On a post it note. On a bunch of post it notes. Focus on these as your goals for the next 2-3 days. You WILL start to feel better. You will start to feel relief.

Make apologies when you're moody with people. Clear your schedule. Acknowledge you've been triggered. Admit to it. Accept it. Own it.

Then - find that point in the distance, beyond your damage and - just start, one foot in front of the other. Or start crawling if you fucking have to.

The Shitty Stories
Except for the first one, which is difficult, but good.

Whether or not you were going to read any of these stories - at least read the first one. It's a story I actually cherish. I was able to record a moment where I broke the intergenerational abuse cycle. I had the humbling privilege of identifying a toxic, unhelpful parental response I was using with my own daughter and then breaking it. On the other side of unfamiliar, I found a level of warmth I had never known from my own mother. I have no idea if I created it, found it or the universe made some random special delivery. But there it was. The story still brings me to tears.

As for the rest of the stories, you're welcome to trash them.

I've made a conscious decision to place all of my painful stories in the same place. If you've heard enough of them, or if you're in a place where it's hard to keep hearing more and more of them, feel free to skip this section. I remember when I craved the stories of other women's past experiences with their mothers. I needed to feel validated; not alone. I needed to be reassured that my mother's cruelty wasn't unique, that it wasn't this extra special abuse meant just for me. What I most desperately needed was confirmation that these events were not so outrageous that they had to be made up in my head. Like she always insinuated (or insisted) they were.

But there came a point where I couldn't hear them any more. I needed to stop indulging in triggers. I had to STOP digging up all of the garbage memories I hated from my past. The ones that would wreck a whole day. The ones that kept me doing chores and household tasks until 11pm just to distract me from them. The ones that kept me in the gym for longer than was healthy. The ones that made therapy so necessary, and made me so angry that I was literally paying for the pain she inflicted. The ones that made me so edgy, and socially awkward and change conversation topics or emotionally attack strangers that reflected anything relating to those memories. The ones that provoked me to smoke 3 cigarettes in a row and dive into a 1.5L bottle of $8.99 red. I had to stop.

I hope you find a point where you're done listening to other people's similar pain. I imagined this stage as being a wheel that kept rocking back and forth in a ditch. You get so close to getting over and past the lip or top of the ledge in front of you, only to roll back, harder, into the ditch. Sometimes rolling back so hard you're scared you're going to wind up going over the edge that's behind you. Fucking scary place to go. But it happens. I needed a way to get forward out of the ditch and stop digging up the memories and reliving the pain. That stage is helpful for a while, but you can't 'live' there. You'll die.

These stories (after the first one) are uncomfortable. They are real. If you relate to them, please remember, you were not supposed to be treated this way - as a child, adult,

Beyond Damage - Julia Gillis - 2019

daughter, or person. These are not healthy interactions between mother and child. They cross boundaries, they betray trust and most of all - they are crazy making. It's not your fault.

Actual Recovery & Letting Go of Your Mother
(And the Parts of you that she fucked up)

I had a really powerful day shortly after the decision to start writing about my experiences of being 'undermothered.' It actually had started the previous day. I was spending a lot of my driving time, to and from work, listening to audiobooks about shitty moms. I was nearing the end of The Emotionally Absent Mother by Jasmin Lee Cori. I hate this book. Not because it's bad, but probably more because it's good. It was uncomfortable, it pointed out a lot of things that were difficult to think about, accept, or work through. But the book really dragged me down, far. We're talking very close to rock bottom.

I was driving back from work to pick up my daughter and listening to one of the last sections when it starts talking about exercises you can do to soothe your damaged inner child or 'unmothered self.' I had turned off the audiobook after picking my daughter up, but the topic was still bothering me. I was emotionally exhausted, deflated, agitated, lost, and unprepared to parent, to be honest. I spent the remainder of the evening giving and receiving attitude with a 3 year old. I actually told my daughter at one point, that I needed a time out for myself. After I got her to bed, I really just felt like a dirty puddle. I felt like a failure as a parent. I looked back on my evening with her. I had tried to start it off fun and it just turned into a lot of negotiating, poor reactions and very little patience for some little human testing boundaries. I didn't feel there was any substance left in myself to make 'present.' And I'm sure she could sense it.

I did a bunch of crying that night after she went to bed. Then more, after I put myself to bed. I tried to continue my reading of Mothers Who Can't Love by Susan Forward but my close friend had texted me and I took the support they were offering. I told them "I'm suffering a lot inside about feeling undermothered. I think I'm going through another layer of realizing I'll never have her back. I'm asking a lot of questions and having a lot of thoughts about how no one can replace her or it's not fair to have others in my life fill the needs that I'm missing by not having her."

I had been noticing a pattern in myself for the past few weeks. The material I had been reading and listening to was holding me in a dark place or perpetuating my unhappiness. I even had a friend suggest this. This was that rolling wheel analogy of being stuck in a shitty place and not being able to move forward.

The next day was my daughter's first day at a brand new preschool program. I vowed the night before to make sure I had a great attitude in the morning, be on time, organized and upbeat for her exciting new day. The morning actually went great. Like - really great. Then I made the better choice of not turning on that fucking audiobook again after dropping her off and heading to work. I knew the books had been putting a damper on my mood and I wanted to keep the 'good parent' feeling I had from that morning's triumph. I picked one of my bluegrass rock playlists and made a point to actually enjoy myself and my thoughts.

That is not what happened.

I made it almost all the way to work and just couldn't keep a lid on it. I have learned over my life to hold back extreme emotional distress - to literally put a cork in it. But this, I could not contain. I had started thinking about my own mother. I thought about my conscious plan to make sure my daughter's first morning of preschool would be awesome for her. Then the comparison of my own mother, and my lack of memories for big, special days she was involved in. Even as a reflective adult, not being able to uncover the special and sweet motherly things that lay hidden until we gain a broader perspective. Because they weren't there; and she didn't do those types of things. The thoughts made me angry at her. Angry about my childhood.

Just as the tears were at the cusp of rolling off my lower lashes, I had to pull the car over. I had to park and white knuckled the steering wheel as my first exhale arched my back and left me breathless. I cringed so hard my face and my abdominal muscles hurt. There was no holding this one back and I just let go. I turned the gas off but left the music on. I actually turned it up louder so I couldn't hear myself choking and coughing on my sobs. I wound up in the fetal position in my seat, curled up, holding my knees and nuzzling my face into the back of my seat, hoping the shape of the seat would imitate a mother's lap and embracing chest.

During this sobbing my mind reached a few places that I can remember. First, my insides felt as though two parts of me were trying to tear apart from one another. It was as if Dr. Jekyll and Mr. Hyde were inside me and attempting to part ways and exit a physical body to become separate entities. It was painful and frightening. As I became aware of this feeling and tried to rationalize what my mind and emotions were doing, I began to understand there was a part of me that was an innocent, vulnerable, sensitive child. This was my unmothered, childhood self; scared and in need. The other half was my adult self; the hardened, highly protected, independent self that was the result of this child not being tended to. Much of my current struggle was based on the theories of leaving behind the painful parts of my past. To reject them and walk away.

I asked myself - which half of myself do I kick out of the car at this moment and leave on the side of the road? After I tear myself in two, who do I drive away from and leave behind? My first instinct was to kick the child out of the car. I thought it made sense to drive away with only my strong self. Of course. Right? But all of the fucking books say to go back and parent that child. Save it. Protect it. They say to go be vulnerable. Go be sensitive. Go form deep, connecting, trusting, raw relationships with people. And it sucked. It fucking sucked realizing that my damaged, defensive, adult solo act was the jaded asshole I was suppose to kick out of the car.

I didn't actually go through with deciding to do that, or going through that thought process. The thought experiment was enough of an epiphany to shock me back into the present. I finally was able to stop crying, wipe my face down, reapply enough makeup to look like all my crying had been done the night before and make it to work for 9am.

I took an hour lunch break that day and connected with a close friend of mine over my 'little episode.' After explaining and talking through a lot of what I had been going through, they made a really interesting suggestion. We were on the topic of trying to get rid of the ideas about life that my mother had hard wired into my brain. This is a major thing that narcissistic mothers do, especially ones that gaslight. They develop your perspective of the world for you and if you attempt to view or explore the world in a way that threatens the reality they've created for you, they use fear tactics to curb you from it. For example: wanting to move out. You want to be free, independant, have your own adult, private space. But they will find any excuse to tell you why that is a horrible, scary and stupid idea. They will say and do anything to make you believe you're not ready, or would fail at living on your own. You may as well just keep living with them (so they can continue to victimize you.)

There were a number of ways that my choices and behavior had been predetermined based on things my mom had taught me about the world. Everything from sex shaming, traveling alone, what other people's achievements and failures meant about them, even basic morality and how to 'be successful.' I started living a really full life at a young age and although I often put my mother's 'facts' about the world to the test, there were many choices I wanted to make for myself, which I didn't. Simply because she had warned me off of them, sternly advising against it, insisting failure and hardship was waiting for me at the end of that choice. Even when there was clear evidence everywhere; flashing neon signs proving her wrong. But I was too scared; scared of breaking our relationship, scared of her possible 'I told you so,' scared of her judgement, criticism, and her potential abandonment of me if I made choices against her suggestions. There were times where I got very head strong about doing things, and she made her pending disappointment very clear. Other times she was a shrieking bully full of threats.

I wanted to get rid of these parts of me. I wanted to get her voice and her views out of my head. I wanted to feel free of her bullshit. This topic also was around my main goal I had started therapy with: I wanted the ability to not be emotionally affected by my mother. I wanted her words, comments, and actions to not feel threatening anymore. I wanted them to be of no consequence; to bare no weight. It took until I was 23 to realize that my mother could lie about things. The concept had never crossed my mind. But after that door had been opened, her words lost integrity all over the place. But she continued to have a choke hold on me even months after I had cut contact with her at 28. Every email, text message, voicemail she sent still provoked me. They provoked insecurity, rage, sadness, fury, disgust, irritation and sometimes fear. I wanted to stop feeling these things about her and her stupid everything. And I wanted the person who I had become, because of her, to be cut out and left on the roadside like the shredded carcass of an illegally hunted stag.

This is when my friend suggested working on parts and pieces. The task of removing or destroying all the pieces of myself that are derivatives of my upbringing by her is too big to accomplish in a fell swoop. Tackling that all at once is suffocating. Why not do it in pieces? Find those misconceptions about the world, and myself, that she's hard wired in and start a checklist. The best way to not be threatened by information from someone is to have confidence in the evidence that they are full of shit.

When I was in my late teens and early 20s, it was a huge goal of mine to get a work visa for England and live there for 6 months. I had traveled there with my grade 12 literature class and loved it. I wanted it so much. I dreamed about it for years and was very determined. As I shared this idea with my mum, I got her typical, disapproving response where she clicks her tongue (also called sucking one's teeth) and carries through with "oh.....Juuuuuliaaaaaa...." She went on to explain that doing that was really not a good idea. That if I got in trouble or anything happened, I would have NO ONE. There would be no one to help me; no family, no friends - I would be all alone. That if I struggled or ran out of money or got lost or couldn't find work, there wouldn't be anyone to help me. That it was seriously unsafe. Why did I want to 'live and work there'? Couldn't I just travel there for a few weeks and come back? There was no reason to stay for six months considering how dangerous and risky that is.

Despite the endless years of evidence and situations where young adults do this all the time....all over the world - the idea became too big for me to follow through on. I actually...fucking...believed her. The idea became uncertain and intimidating. Had she ever done this? No. Do other people do this all the time? Yes. Do other people sometimes fail and get stuck? Yes. Does this become some sort of horrific situation they can't sort out themselves? Rarely.

Why. The. Fuck - did I allow her stupid, inexperienced comments to squash this dream of mine? Because: gaslighting. Because: control. Because: victims of narcissistic mothers are just little Stockholm Syndrome victims walking around with their heads involuntarily shoved up their asses. They literally think the world is just one big colon and mother controls entry and exit of everything. You literally have to push your way out if you want to get your own view of the real world.

So the exercise derived from the actual healthy conversation I was describing before my rant: Make a list of the things my mother taught me about the world and myself.

Write down what I actually feel and believe. Write down experiences I've had that prove her wrong. Again and again and again. The list of bullshit she's fed me is endless. Everything from sex shaming to insisting that my daughter NEEDS all 4 of her grandparents in her life. Or her comment that I'm the only one in the world who doesn't appreciate unsolicited advice. Literally - the only person in the world who reacts poorly to it. I'm the only person on the entire planet that feels a random hovering stranger approaching me with commentary and advice on what I'm doing is intrusive and rude. Right. The only person ever.

Flash forward to later in the evening on that same day. My daughter had fallen asleep in the car after her huge, special day (where she was so awesome and brave!) When she does this, I park the car on the back lawn and roll down all the windows. I'm able to see her sleeping in the car, out the back door, while I tidy the kitchen and bring all our stuff in from the car. She woke up a little fussy and distressed (understandable - I don't like waking up strapped into a car seat either...) So I carried her inside, got her some cold water and just sat with her on my lap in the living room, waiting for her to calm. This didn't happen. Her whimpers turned into crying. I kept my cool pretty well and worked with positive distractions like asking if she wanted me to read her favorite story in my robot voice that she finds funny. Not working. Then I started talking about positive parts of her day and a cute situation one of the daycare workers told me about. That worked for a moment, but she wouldn't carry on the story with me and started crying again. I started trying to work with encouraging her to take deep breaths. She got a moment of gag reflect and I reminded her that when she cries too hard, she starts to vomit and gently insisted she calm down. She asked me to take her to the potty in between her jagged, crying gasps. I carried her to the bathroom and set her down asking her if she wanted help pulling her shorts off. She said no and stomped her feet at me, then she put seat up and leaned forward over the toilet! As thought she knew that's where to wait to be ready to puke.

She grabbed my hands and put them on her chest so I was hugging her from behind. My dad had talked to me a lot about this 'butterfly tapping' technique that is supposed to help children learn to self sooth. I've tried it with my daughter a few times, but never got anywhere with it. My tactic when she gets worked up and cries hard is to encourage her to breath with me, take deep breaths and talk to her about being calm. At this point, leaning over the toilet as she continued to cry, I tried tapping her chest softly with my fingers and counting 3 taps, then saying 'breath in, breath out' and repeating this. We weren't getting anywhere. She didn't like the counting, she didn't catch on with my breathing. Her crying was increasing. My cool was decreasing.

Simply encouraging or even insisting that she calm down was a useless fucking answer to this.

I can't remember which one of us eventually decided that was enough of that bullshit but I wound up sitting on the floor of the bathroom, leaning against the wall with her curled into my lap and my arms around her. Her head was nuzzled into my chest, soaking my bare chest and shirt.

I gave in. I had no more tools for this. I was lost as a parent.

She was this little, innocent, tired, overstimulated 3 year old. She had a huge day with new things and I fucking know what it's like to just need a good cry and have some catharsis. So I rubbed her back and starting saying things like: "It's ok. I love you. I'm here for you. I'll always be here for you. I'll keep you safe. I'll always protect you. Everything's going to be ok. I won't go anywhere. I'll never leave you. I'll be here as long as you need." Words I never heard as a child.

I just repeated all of these things. Again and again. Until the tears became less. And the jagged breathing smoothed out. I let her wipe her runny nose all over my bare chest and shirt. I let her hair get messy. I held her tight and kept rubbing her back until she slowly lifted her head off my chest and sat up in my lap. On her own. When she was good and ready.

It didn't take long into my 'mantra help' before I realized I had a real, live child for me to mother...the way I wanted to be mothered. All those stupid exercises about carrying around a doll and mothering your inner child the way you wished you would have been mothered....I had an opportunity. In my arms. Right in front of me. I didn't have to pretend. I can offer her all of the loving things that I missed out on. I was already doing that with her all the time. But this moment was tense and I didn't have anything to go on. My crying when I was young was responded to with the first tactics I started with. Being told to calm down, insistence that I self regulate, a stern or firm suggestion that I breathe, stop crying and verbally communicate what was wrong so we could find a solution. I was taught to 'collect myself,' and if I was struggling to accomplish this...the insistence became more harsh. Who the fuck does that? Tells a kid they have to stop crying and 'get it together'? Its fucking sick. After I would stop crying, if I couldn't explain 'why' I was crying, I was told that there was nothing that could be done for me. "I can't help you if you can't tell me what's wrong."

Telling my daughter all of those loving things - those special things a mother is supposed to say to their innocent, helpless, needy, scared, tired child, made me feel so good. They made me feel like I was giving her exactly what she needed. And I selfishly shared that moment. I imagined that I was her, getting the love I missed out on. Being told by my mother that everything was going to be ok, that she was there to protect me, that she would never leave and that she loves me. Just being present with me for the tears, rubbing my back and not telling me that I 'had to calm down.'

Big parenting win. Huge. Also a big win for my damaged, angry, lonely inner child. I do that a lot I think. When I'm parenting my daughter, I ask my younger self "How would I have liked to be treated in this situation?" It steers me right just about every time.

This is where you can stop. If you want.
The rest of these stories - don't have a positive ending.
Until years later.

Story 1:

When I was still small enough (but not really - I think I was still doing this at 6, 7, 8...I can't remember when it stopped) I would cling to the front of her while she made dinner in the kitchen. She would usually let me up and just wear me on her front, with my legs wrapped around her waist, feet hooked behind her back and arms around her neck. I would just cling to her. She would keep making dinner, or keep doing whatever task she was doing in the kitchen. She would eventually tell me to get off, or that I was getting too heavy. At the time, I was simply happy to have the physical contact. I was getting something from her. I was grateful.

Looking back on it, I can see how much damage this created. There are no memories of her stopping or pausing to embrace me back. I don't ever remember her 'hugging me back.' I was literally the monkey on her front. She was tolerating me. She was allowing the contact. After months or years of this after school/after work routine of her coming home and starting dinner and me craving the attention and affection - she never made a change. She never instigated a '20 minutes of connecting' time when she got home. Or worked out a time 'for us' where I could get what I felt I was missing - she never considered this a need from her that wasn't being filled for me. She just kept dealing with my clinginess, until she could really insist that I was 'too big/heavy/old' for it. Or until I learned to start rejecting her back.

Digging deep, I can maybe remember that there were times where she would step out of the kitchen to actually look at the news on the tv, that was always on before (and during) dinner. It's a vague memory that she may have stood and swayed back and forth gently, as mothers unconsciously do when holding their child. At this point she may have finally wrapped her hands under my bum to hold me up and support me. I'm not sure if those translucent memories are real. I have no idea. Those moments may have happened - or maybe I just hope they did. They certainly aren't the dominant recollection.

Story 2:

The repeated nights at the dinner table where my oldest brother bullied me and she did nothing. There was a routine at the dinner table almost every night until my oldest brother left for university. I always remember him at the head of the table. Even my parents would sit, squished in together, on the opposite end. I remember him also always serving himself first. I have some sort of odd recollection that since he was 'the biggest' he was allowed to claim as much food as he needed first, then all of the rest of us would serve ourselves. There was a family dynamic that put him at the top of the pecking order. He was the Golden Child.

Every night we all sat at the table as a family, the 5 of us. Most of those nights I got picked on by my oldest brother. It didn't matter what I spoke up about. If I had a question, or a story about my day - he found a way to make me feel stupid, inadequate, ridiculous. It was pointed out with harshness. He was 5 years older than me. There was no competition. But I was picked on, as though I should be at his level of intelligence. The worst part was my mother's response.

It was an irritated "Andrew!" The tone was a rather forced and disingenuous chastising.

Not a warning. It was just a one word exclamation. And his petulant "what?!" His tone saying "I'm not doing anything wrong!" He would stare her down and furrow his brow. The table would go silent. Nothing more would be done.

This went on for years. He was never punished. He was never encouraged to treat me better or with more understanding. No matter how many nights a week I got shamed, picked on, insulted, cut down, ridiculed - there was nothing more than an irritated warning. No justice. I learned my mother was not invested in protecting me. From anything.

Story 3:

I begged her, at a young age, that I really wanted to start dance lessons or dance class. I wanted so badly to wear the outfit and glide around in slippers. I wanted the bun and the tutu. I wanted to feel like a graceful swan. I saw the elegance.

Her response was that it required a lot of dedication. She told me dance was a difficult commitment to take on. That people who get involved in dance have to put in a lot of time and effort. I recall other comments about 'those women's bodies' having injuries and issues later, and a cap on their career. I was between the ages of 6-8. I had no idea what she was talking about.

But the undertone was that she didn't approve and it was unlikely that I would be successful at it. That part was clear. I never revisited that discussion with her. I was too young to argue for it. And I knew continuing to beg or demanding wouldn't go well. If she even gave in, she would point out every failure and reaffirm every hardship as the reason I should have never asked her to let me go. Looking back on this story helped me put the pieces together about a mother's jealousy. I was often deterred from activities and experiences that she didn't have access to, or success in, from her own life.

Story 4:

"Mom, I'm ready to go." I would stand at the crossroads between the living room, dining room and hallway. No reaction, no acknowledgement. Just the gentle turning of the next magazine page, as though she hadn't heard me. As though there was no child that existed to be driven somewhere. She furthered the control by calmly rising from her seat, gracefully making her way to the bathroom, and touching up her makeup. I don't think I ever badgered her. "C'mon, I'm going to be late" wasn't a 'thing.' If I ever tried this - I'm sure it was met with a stern talking to in the car about how unappreciated she was, how she needed time to herself sometimes, since she's such a hard working, devoted mother.

But I know there were sections of time where I chose to help her by getting her coat out of the closet for her, or carrying something by the door to the car (her purse, the grocery bins, whatever she needed for her errands) and being ready and waiting in the car for her. Or the opposite where I simply stated I was ready and would meet her in the car. I would sit, waiting, angrily for her to glide out - and met with a very silent and cold car ride to...wherever.

This wasn't sometimes. This was always. I was never dropped off with "Have fun at practice!" The drive never included conversations like "It's so cool you got chosen as the youth rep for City Counsel, how's that going?" It was a silent understanding that I was infringing on her life by having one of my own. I almost always was given a ride. But I paid for every single one of them. The cost was having to sit in her pool of contempt for me. She liked me best when I was quiet, at home, joining her hobbies.

Story 5:

"Mom - I think I got my period." I call out of the open bathroom door and down the hall. There's silence for a few seconds. "Is that ok? Or do you need to stay home from school?" "Uh, I think I'm fine. I'll go." Then I think there was some indication or reminder of where her pads/tampons/feminine products were. That was really the extent of that. There's nothing more to that story. We didn't discuss anything else.

It wasn't a special moment. No bonding. Flat, clinical, unimportant. I remember other friends telling me their moms and aunts or cousins threw fun/funny tampon parties for them, or at least there was some sort of womanhood celebration. It became a right of passage, or even just an excuse for a little party. I spent a lot of time growing up, telling myself "I don't need that" in regards to special things other girls got with their moms. My defense. Shrug it off. Be nonchalant. Nothing is painful if you make it not a big deal. I adopted this concept with most other things in my life. Expect nothing and you'll never be jilted or disappointed.

Story 6:

Getting time with her meant taking on her hobbies. On weekends or during the summer when my mom would need to make trips into town or the city, I was given choices.

Either come with her, or be dropped somewhere else (or be left at home, when I was old enough.) I would be informed that she was dropping off geology samples and either attending an antique show, or second hand shopping for something specific. Sometimes in town it was a trip to the library. These were things for her. Things she wanted to do and enjoyed. Which is fine. Every parent needs those things.

But it was the imbalance I realized, with reflection. Growing up, I was aware of my feelings of neglect. So for much of my later childhood and preteen years I learned how to go antique shopping. I learned how to sew, knit, garden, and get really good at 5000 piece puzzles. I also got very good at identifying high-end brand name clothing and assessing its quality in thrift stores. All because it meant I could spend time with my mother. My other option was being without her. Or alone. Getting no 'extra' attention.

Going to the library was always for her own hunt. Whatever project she was working on. I was directed to find my own book section of interest, and meet her back at a specified point or to come find her. This trip wasn't about sharing. We were not finding books 'together.' I was tagging along. Though I can't complain about this one. I am now an avid (obsessive?) reader. I wouldn't be caught dead without a book at my bedside, in my purse or on my phone, at a cafe, on a plane, in a waiting room. That's not damage - that's just good breeding.

I remember all of the times I was dropped off at my cousins' houses instead. Those days were filled with Aunt Chris or Aunt Chrissy taking us to the movie theater, the wave pool, to White Spot for burgers and fries, to the petting farms, for a nature walk, to big parks with new jungle gyms, and other destination spots, filled with other kids and families. I loved those memories. But not with my mother - because she didn't do those things.

While I still had a relationship with my mother, I kept her hobbies. Even in my own time. Having personal projects that aligned with her hobbies gave us something to connect about. But after I cut her out - I realized I hated shopping. All kinds of shopping. Perusing, window shopping, thrift shopping, spending hours just 'puttering.' I hate owning things and I hate wasting my time, looking at things I 'want' but don't need. I don't knit or sew as a hobby. I actively avoid it. My mother and I used to buy clothes that were 'almost right.' We would take them home and spend hours together altering, restitching and adding to the garments. I don't buy anything that needs to be altered now. Not ever. I never spend time in my garden. I don't even want to. I roll my eyes at the fact that I 'have' a garden. My true preference being an apartment, with a nonexistent lawn, which never needs to be mowed and weeds that never need to be weeded.

I make every Sunday for my daughter, who chooses what we do that day. Park, swimming pool, the beach, meeting with friends, petting farms and even 'latte dates.' She gets a half-sweet hot chocolate at 'her temperature' and we just sit and talk. 4-year olds say the coolest things. Sometimes we just go to the dollar store and I let her pick out party &

craft supplies. We go home and spend the entire day making crafts and filling the living room with balloons.

I have tons of other hobbies that I find enjoyable and spend time indulging in. And I don't make my daughter explore red wine with me. But she joins me for live concerts and hikes when its age appropriate. And when I go to the library, I have the ones I want waiting for me on the pick up shelf, having requested them on the library site ahead of time. If my daughter is with me - we're there to find books for her. Together.

Story 7:

I remember by the age of 14, I had moved my bedroom to one of the basement rooms. One night I was sobbing loudly in my bed, downstairs in the back corner of the house. It was late at night and everyone in the house had gone to bed. I remember sobbing louder, hoping my mom upstairs would hear me. I would listen for her door to open and to hear her footsteps down the hall and staircase. They weren't coming. I wanted her to hear me so badly. I forced myself out of bed and curled up on one of the bottom steps and continued to sob loudly. Hoping my crying would make it up the staircase and down the hall, through her closed door. Finally - I hear her door. She comes to me and sits beside me on the step above, putting an arm around my shoulders.

"Pookie, what's wrong?"

Through choking sobs I say "I feel like your love is conditional."

"Oh, sweetie, my love isn't conditional. But my support is."

I remember being confused. I didn't ask about her level of support. Just her love. I remember crying harder after she said this. Then more, as she continued to hold me and further explain 'why' her support is conditional. We must have had an argument earlier in the night about her not supporting something I was doing. But her explanation was not prompted. There was no comfort from this. The topic of her love being unconditional was not touched on further during the discussion that I remember.

At the end, I don't remember a bonding moment between mother and daughter. I don't remember feeling warmed by her. I remember crawling back inside myself and learning yet again, I do not go to my mother when I'm looking for love, comfort and compassion. I went to bed with thicker walls that night. A reaffirmation to not 'trust in mother.' Do not seek her out.

The bitterness of this story carried on for years. I will never forget that moment. Sometimes the pain comes not from what is added in, but from what is left out. Her love being unconditional.

Story 8:

   When I was in grade 12, about to graduate high school, I was more than ready to move out. I had begged for boarding school growing up, I had read articles about teenagers who had successfully divorced their parents. I remember this was how I learned the word *emancipated*. I wanted to be separate from them; I wanted to be 'away.' During highschool I regularly worked 2 part time jobs outside of school hours. Despite my heavy drinking on weekends, I was able to tuck away $3,000 by graduation. I knew I could use this for travel...and finally getting out. My mother was adamant that I not be allowed to move out until I finished high school. After all of the trouble, the fighting, the drinking, the yelling, the running away - she still didn't want me out. She didn't want me to leave. I hated my home. But somehow, I still felt I needed her permission to leave.

   Graduating from highschool, in my mind, symbolized the end of her legal control for me. And I had made my exit plans. I was looking for apartments with my boyfriend, and going to viewings. It started a few months before school ended. I could even pay my half of rent while not living there, if my boyfriend and I could find one before I graduated, and he could move in first.

   I noticed as I got closer to my final days of school and closer to finding a place of my own, my mother became more agitated, anxious and would bring up objections more frequently. She tried many angles, from me being too young, to it being a lot of responsibility, to (her) facts that a lot of young adults can't afford living on their own at this age. Her main argument being that moving in with a 'boyfriend first' was a really bad decision. If we break up, the rental agreement could get really complicated. Relationships at this age don't last very long, she pointed out. Someone could get stuck with the entire rent. I ignored her - obviously.

   I finally chose an apartment, 7 minutes down the road from my parents. At some point, during my final month of school, we were arguing about it. Again. I finally hit an apex. We were fighting so passionately she had pulled off the road and into a parking lot for us to duke it out. I screamed at her "What is this really about?! Why is this such a hard thing for you?! Is this a youngest bird leaving the nest thing?" I was tired of all her passive aggressive attempts to deter me and wanted her to just come out with it.

   "No! No - that's not it!"
   "Then what!?"
   "I'm worried you're going to accidentally get pregnant, decide to keep it, and ruin your life." She blurted.

   I was shocked. This made no sense. 1) I hated kids. At this point in my life - I never wanted to have children. Not ever. 2) I had a full plan for myself, my life and my career. I was taking a year off to relax and travel and have fun, then get right into a bachelor's degree. No excuses. I made this plan. I was keeping this plan. 3) Not only did I know how to use contraceptive, I had been on it for years. 4) I was full blown, feminist, women's lib, pro choice. If i didn't want it, I wasn't having it.

I burst into tears. I was so angry at her for having such a low opinion of my ability to have control of my own life. As though things could get so out of hand for me so easily. As though all the years of my stubborn, driven, laser focus personality would just fly out the window if I moved out of her house, and in with a boyfriend. I got out of the car and stormed off. I walked 3-4 blocks to my close friends apartment. All of my friends were there, including my best girl friend and my boyfriend. I told them everything.

My best friend says "Well the real questions is why the fuck does your mom think that you having a kid will ruin your life? Is that how she feels about having kids?"

I still find myself conflicted over this memory. Is that really what she was worried about? If so - the implications are sickening. The WASP mentality, the hatred of her own life as a mother, her low opinion of my ability to handle life as an adult. If this was simply a distraction tactic - I can't imagine how sickening the truth would sound. Losing access to her favorite victim in the family. How watching me succeed at being on my own, would shake her own ego. I don't know which is worse.

Story 9:
When I got into university, it was a big deal. For me - as well as for my mother, apparently. I had worked really hard to get into a really selective program. You have to go through a portfolio interview process. Anywhere from 75 to 145 people apply every year. Only 20 get accepted every year. I actually didn't get in at first. I was 2nd down on the waitlist incase any of the 20 selected didn't accept. But I got the call.

I both loved and hated my first year. I loved university, and I loved learning the content. But just that taste of the outside world opened my eyes a lot. After my first year I was able to see that the industry I was training for wouldn't make me happy. I wanted to keep going to school, but I wanted to switch to general studies and start carving a new path. So when my mom did an 'end of first year' check in phone call, I told her that I enjoyed it, but wanted to explore some other programs at a different university. She was surprised at first. My grades had been so good and I talked about how much I liked it.

So I explained further; that I saw where the program would take me and I didn't want to do that with my life. She replied, being a bit more firm, telling me I should at least give it another year. I countered and explained what else I would like to be doing instead. Then she became down right insistent.

"If you quit this program, all the money will stop." She said. I weighed my options. It actually made me anxious as fuck. I thought through having to work while going to school to pay for everything. I thought about just going to work with no post secondary education. I thought about having to come out of school with student loans and being in debt for years. Those ideas paralyzed me. I know other people do it every day. But I had no fucking skills or coping mechanisms for that life. I knew I wouldn't survive.

Then we did this every summer. After my second year, we had the round up call again. My grades were great again; something like a 3.8 GPA. She was shocked again - at my matter of fact "I still don't like it and want to leave." Her excuse this time, "But you're half way done!" When I pressed this time, she was shrill. She told me that no one would hire someone with an unfinished bachelor's degree. Employers would wonder where 2 years of my life went, if I had no record of that time. She convinced me that NO ONE hires a quitter. People who drop out of university are seen as unreliable and have no follow through. And I believed her. That fucking gaslighting bully.

I completed my third year. We had the call again. But this point my indignation and snarky attitude gave me pleasure. But she was warmer. "You only have one more year to go!" It pleased her so much. It's as if she didn't hear me when I explained that I would be doing nothing with this degree. I told her flat out, that I would not be looking for work in my degree field.

The best part came when I finally graduated. We were celebrating a grouping of birthdays and other triumphs on my mom's side of the family. I was sitting at my grandmother's huge wooden table. My mother's oldest sister turns to me and asks, "So, Julia, have you thought about which firms you'll be applying to?"

I looked at her and said "Actually, I've accepted a job as a Chef at a restaurant in Gastown. I'm not applying to any firms and I'm not going into Interior Design. You're sister wasted $60,000 on an education I told her year after year, that I didn't want."

I said it loud enough for my mother to hear. In a room full of all the people she fears judgement from.

Story 10:
The day I told her that Ryan and I were planning to get pregnant was stressful. The build up was nerve wracking, and it ended in a whisper, not a bang. She was sitting at my dining room table, on a beautiful sunny afternoon.

I said, "wait here, I have something to tell you." I went into the bedroom and collected the 'expecting baby' books Ryan and I had collected and the one Celtic Baby Names book we could agree on. I brought them to the table and laid them out in front of her, like a project for her to assess.

She looked over the covers and titles. She very calmly says "Oh, well you're 24. So that's about the right time."

I was waiting for her shock. Her surprise. Her happiness. Even a fight - would have been better than her nonchalant, no-big-deal, this is nothing special attitude. I was utterly deflated. The day that I announced to my mother I was starting my journey to make my own family - is overcast by her sheer lack of response.

Story 11: Miscarriage & Mismothering

My mother took me out for coffee some time shortly after I had miscarried my first pregnancy. I was grieving hard and she hadn't been much help in the process. She tried in her own way, but it was clinical and cold. She offered books on grieving miscarriage and suggested library trips to get them. She repeatedly told me to call and talk to my aunt that had suffered through many of them (though that aunt had never disclosed that to me herself.) But genuine words from my own mother on how to heal and find recovery were lacking. I don't recall warmth from her.

On our coffee date, we sat down with our tea and she starts with something like: ""There are some things I need to tell you about your father."

The next part I remember crystal clear. She explained that my dad was not taking the recent loss (my miscarriage) very well. He was grieving a lot and he's been very upset. It's been very hard for him to deal with, on top of his PTSD. And - that she has recently discovered that he's been having an affair.

I sat and stared at her. Speechless. My eyes welled up. I started crying. My brain had short circuited.

The beginning of the conversation and the end molded together and I meekly asked, "Is this my fault?"

It was a genuine question at the time. I truly thought I had heard her explain that my recent miscarriage had affected my father in some way, to such great pain on top of his complex PTSD, that it had caused him to start cheating on her.

She breezed by her "of course not? Why would you think that?" and continued to explain his dissociative issues, forgetting that he ever had a family and that she was his wife. She went into detail about all the facts she had complied and her diagnosis. She went over all of his PTSD symptoms again, as I cried softly. Then she added in everything she knew about the affair.

A week or so after my torture coffee - my mother and I had a phone call. She adds one last thing to the conversation: "Also, I just thought I should mention, when I told you about your father's affair, you asked if it was your fault. I'm a little concerned about where that came from. You might want to bring that up with your grief counselor."

Story 12:

At some point, early in my pregnancy, my mother and I made a trip together out into the Okanagan of BC. There was a place called Gallaghar Lake Lodge, just outside of Oliver. I loved this place. I had 2 summer vacations there. I can't be sure of which years. Once in my preteens and again when I was in my early teens. I was invited to go with my cousins. My own family didn't take summer trips anywhere together. So this was a special treat.

My mom and I decided to get some bonding time and take a trip out there for a few nights. During the drive out - I made the mistake of finally telling her that Ryan (my daughter's father) and I, had eloped - 2 years prior. We were talking - and bonding - and connecting - and sharing. So I felt it would be a nice to share this. The novelty had worn off anyway. Big fucking mistake. At this point I still hadn't put the pieces together that her MO was taking any information I give her and turning it around on me later. She took it well at the time. I don't remember how the conversation ended or molded into the next topic... but I thought it went pretty well because we breezed through it. She admitted she was surprised, but nothing imploded. I remember explaining, that at some point, I was going to put the photos from the elopement together and have albums printed to give to family members. That Ryan and I would tell people eventually. But in our own way.

We didn't talk about it the rest of the trip that I can remember. But I sure as fuck rememeber what happened after we returned home. It took less than a week for her to 'stop by' for a visit, with my father in tow. She sat down, while my father stayed standing. I think they both kept their jackets and shoes on. This wasn't out of the ordinary, to be honest.

But then she says it: "You have something to tell your father."

I was whole-heartedly confused in the moment. She could see my bewilderment and continued, "About you and Ryan."

I had honestly forgotten I had told her at all. She had given it just enough time for me to carry on and believe it wasn't a big deal. But she was going to make me pay. For getting married without telling her. For allowing some of our friends to be there and not her. For not letting her be involved. My bewilderment turned into a scorched earth glare. Her stone cold poker face was impeccable. Her gaze challenged me to refuse; after my dad now knows I have something to 'fess up.' My dad stood there, now alone in the bewilderment - having no idea what he had been dragged into. She was cornering me into admitting that Ryan and I had eloped 2 years prior to my dad. She wasn't going to tell him - I had to. She was treating me like a child, being forced to confess my 'wrong-doing to daddy.' I had hurt her and she wanted to punish me.

My dad shrugged. He offered a pleasant congratulations. I was angry and sullen. But blind to how much worse it was about to get. This wasn't the end.

Story 13:

The day before moving from Vancouver to Vancouver Island, at 4 and a half months pregnant, my mother took it upon herself to announce my elopement to her entire side of the family. Without warning and without permission.

We got together to celebrate a few birthdays and to offer a bon voyage to Ryan and I before our move in 2 days. I hear the clinking of a champagne glass and see my mother at the head of the table. She begins with congratulating our pregnancy and wishing us good luck on our move, then mentions there is another announcement concerning Ryan and I that she would like to share. I look at her, then look at Ryan - and it only takes me a second put the pieces together.

"Mum, no." I whisper from 5 feet away. "Oh fuck no," I hear Ryan say under his breath beside me.
My mum looks at me quickly and pauses, then continues.
"Mum, don't," I say lounder. "Yes Julia," she counters.
"Mum, stop it!" I say louder. I hear comments around the table of "what's going on..."
"Shhhhhh," she chides me.

"Ryan and Julia are married...for the past 2 years..." she carried on about being happy to finally celebrate it and share it with the family. I put on an obviously fake smile. Ryan was fuming beside me and keeping his mouth very shut. We took the kind jokes about being able to keep it on lock down for so long, and the happy wishes from the other family members.

Before we left, I had thoroughly chewed my mom out. I left in a rage. I told her that it was NOT ok that she did that. I had not given her permission to share it with family. She insisted that I had mentioned she was 'allowed to tell people.' I couldn't remember if I had said that or not, but I sure as fuck know it's not polite to announce someone elses elopement for them, without warning.

It didn't end there. I got text messages later after getting home. She questioned my behavior, demanded I explain why I was angry with her and offered a list of reasons why she had done nothing for me to be angry about. I remember doing a relatively good job at explaining that regardless of what she 'thinks,' her actions were disrespectful and that she owes Ryan and I an apology. It fell on deaf ears. She dug her heels in and continued to demand a logical explanation for my anger towards her. I couldn't repeat myself any clearer. Any reason I offered was simply swatted away.

It didn't end there. (Yes, twice. There's more.) Ryan and I held a moving party with our friends the next day. We offered pizza and beer to anyone who showed up to help us load the truck. My mother - showed up unannounced and demanded a private audience with me. She waltzed in like Queen of Sheba. While our friends were crawling all over our house, moving boxes and furniture in and out of doorways, she thought this was a good time to show up and duke it out - and she knew damn well they were all going to be there.

She carried on the exact conversation with me. She dug deep, demanding explanations for my anger, twisting my words, questioning why I didn't have a wedding with family involved in the first place. She stretched the span of the argument to include huge web of issues between us. The argument spilled from the empty bedroom I had shut us in, to the kitchen as I got fed up with circling accusations over who instigated the original problem. I remember shouting at her, "I'm not doing this with you right now! You can't BE here." My friends were all over the 900 square foot house, catching snippets of our humourless farce.

It finally took its nose dive when I said, "See! This is why I don't tell you things!"

She shrieks back, "Oh! So this is MY fault?!" Tears well up in her eyes as they widen.

I'm shocked into silence. I realize there is no point. I realize she has come here for nothing but to dominate my time. This entire visit has been a ruse. Whatever twisted, fucked up, damaged, subconscious reaction she had to me being angry with her - has become a monster and she's brought it into my house. I tell her to get out. I tell her to leave. And after she leaves, I cry on my back steps. I become surrounded by my girl friends, with loving arms around me. I tell them what happened. My friend Lisa tells me that no mom should treat their daughter that way.

Story 14:
I remember the days around giving birth to my daughter. My mom and dad came to stay with us around the due date. I was having strong braxton-hicks contractions for a few days - but even then, I called them too early. They were with us for nearly 5-7 days before I finally gave birth. I had a home birth and I remember my mother in the room, as I started to bare down, holding on to the back headboard and trying to breath through it.

"Your not breathing properly Julia," she said sternly. "I'm trying!" I snapped back. She picks extra special moments for critical feedback.

Like later that day, when I got up to make myself breakfast. At the time I didn't think anything of it. I had labored for 13 hours, gotten up to take a shower, breast fed and then rested with my newborn. When I woke up hungry, I simply got up to make myself food. I'm just that person. I want or need something, I just go get it. (I later resented being in a house with my mom, my dad and my husband and not one of them offered to bring me or make me food. 12 hours after having a home birth...fuckers.)

As I fry my eggs, they start to stick and get mangled. The pan was cast iron, I was still groggy and didn't have the finesse with the oil and heat to keep them from sticking. I didn't really care. I needed food, not a gourmet meal. But my mother chooses to lean over my shoulder and peer into the pan. Then she looked at me and snickered. It was a scoff and laugh mixed together. She looks at me and says something really fucking condescending and rhetorical, like "didn't use enough oil?" With a bully's goading smile. I remember her eyes being bright, as though the 'teasing moment' would be appreciated by both of us. I wanted to sear the skin off her face at the moment.

She put a cherry on the cake when the midwife did her 24 hour after check-in. My midwife and I were on the couch, my newborn spread out on the middle seat cushion between us as she checked temperature and heartbeat. I began to dress her into a pj onesie. Just as I begin to shimmy her adorable little arm down one sleeve my mother peaks over the back of the couch to observe.

"Julia, why are you doing that the hard way? Don't you know to scrunch up the sleeve and just pop the hand through?" Again, she laughs at me. Again, I want to sear the skin off her face.

Story 15: The Mother's Day Massacre
The first Mother's Day after my daughter was born was the last time I celebrated Mother's Day with my mother. It was the last time I ever called her to wish her a happy Mother's Day. It was awful - truly, painfully horrific. I remember 3 things from this trip: Jane instructing me to monitor my husband's future fathering ability, getting a '4 generations' photo with my grandmother, my mother, myself and my daughter, and my mother being fucking delusional.

After she had picked up me from the ferry, I remember driving along the highway above West Vancouver. I remember where we were exactly, just approaching the exit for Park Royal and heading for Lion's Gate Bridge to go see my Grandmother at UBC. We were (of course) discussing my Dad. My mom loves explaining how and why he's sick, she's the expert on this. All of his 'Adult Child of an Alcoholic' issues mixed with his Dissociative PTSD issues and all of his current symptoms that make him a broken man and parent; it was her favorite topic for the better part of 5 years.

Then out of nowhere, she says: "Because of Ryan's upbringing that's something you'll have to watch for with him as well."

I replied with something like: Sorry? Or: Excuse me?

She tries again: "Well from what you've told me about Ryan's mum, when he was young, you'll need to watch Ryan for some of the same things, as a father."

I'm going to count myself lucky because I think I was already mad at her for a previous disagreement (within the last week or month) and had my defenses up. My mind did a lot of things very quickly before I replied. I first realized that she believed that she had to supervise my Dad's parenting all his life to make sure he was 'doing it right.' Then thinking forward about having to manage and supervise my own husband's parenting due to (her insinuation that) his upbringing being less than her version of perfect.

Somewhere, I found enough good sense and power to set her straight. I actually read her the riot act on this one. I replied by explaining that Ryan has self awareness about his upbringing, which we discuss openly and **both** work at helping each other be the parents we hope to be. Also that Ryan is 'my husband' and she doesn't get to make comments about me controlling or monitoring him as a developing father. Him and I are on the same team and its not my responsibility to watch over him. I then carried on to point out that everyone has an upbringing that affects how they parent. I turned it around on her in an instant and asked if she thought her upbringing allowed her to be a perfect parent. I'm not sure if she realized it before she said it....but she did more than just shoot herself in the foot. She dropped an atom bomb on herself.

She replied by explaining that her and her siblings mostly parented themselves. Her own mum wasn't involved with raising them enough to pass down any generational abuse to cause her to have any problems with being a fully competent parent.

Parented themselves? That's neglect. That's emotional abuse. That's a nice, giant, 3 ton elephant in the room. And she thinks it's a spider in the corner. Fucking delusional. And I told her so.

We had a second disagreement that same day. I got on the topic of how rude it was to offer unsolicited advice to strangers. I pointed out that when she does that, people actually don't like it. She told me "that's a 'you' thing, Julia."

I gave it some room. "Ok, I can understand that there are people out there that probably really appreciate that. They are struggling with something or confused and are too shy or nervous to ask for help. So it's nice when someone steps in and helps. But there is a whole other half of the population that finds it rude, presumptuous, unnecessary and intrusive. Not to mention condescending."

Her response: "No Julia! That's just you! No one else treats being helped, as negatively as you do. You have such a huge problem accepting help and you need to get over it."

Beyond Damage - Julia Gillis - 2019

I had to laugh at this. The concept of me being 1 in 7 billion - that didn't appreciate it when people offer unsolicited advice. Sure.

Story 16:

I've had one mother-daughter therapy session. It was a straight wreck. The entire session was her manipulative bullshit. She gushed about how hard she fought for me when I was younger - for people to let 'me be me.' She demanded that I give her the reason I started to become distant when I was 14. She accused me of becoming my 14 year old self again, at the age of 25 - as the reason for our current mother-daughter relationship problems. She sang bleeding hearts about my dad being sick and how hard that's been on her and how horrible I've been to her through the whole process. Then we would circle back to "what could I have possibly done that was so horrible to you, for you to resent me so much."

It took me so long to learn that abuse mechanism. Every answer I gave, every painful memory I shared, was argued against. After disproving or discrediting my answer, she would circle back. The goal was to dissolve the entire list, until I had no memories left unshared and unrefuted. The final analysis would be that she had never done anything to cause such malice in her direction - therefore I should stop having it.

Where we got to the nitty gritty was my relationship with her sister-in-law. My favorite aunt, whom she felt had stolen her place as my mother. She mocked my aunt, particularly for her personality trait of being enthusiastically complementary of others. My aunt showers people with supportive language and positive reinforcement. I explained it matter of factly - that lots of people enjoy being spoken to that way, they find it encouraging, helpful and comforting. It's a 'nice' way to talk to someone else.

My mother was shocked. "You NEEEEEDDDD that!?" she screamed at me, half unseating herself from the couch, lunged in my direction.

"Yes. Tons of people do! And it fucking sucks when I've wished all my life to hear you say those things to me, my own mother, and I have to go somewhere else to get it!"

She pounded her chest with her closed fist for each word she shrieked: "I. Don't. Have. That. Language."

Clearly. Her eyes glossed with tears. The drama. The yelling. Her false emotions to make a flashy show in front of the therapist mixed with her true pain. I could see it. It was so evident. My mother had never had supportive, encouraging, kind, positive language offered to her growing up. She saw my desire for it and me getting it as both a weakness in me, and a looking glass into her own jealousy.

Story 17:
When my mom and I would fight I would come out of the conversation not being able to repeat back the conversation to someone else. I couldn't organize a play by play. No summary or synopsis. I wouldn't even be able to explain what exactly we were fighting about and my side of the debate versus hers. My partner of 7 years would ask me what happened and I would struggle to explain what started the argument, why I got upset and how the conclusion of the conversation came about. I either couldn't give it any linear qualities or actually couldn't remember much of what was said. Yet I was deeply affected, upset and in a rather tumultuous state.

I look back on this and realize these were probably dissociative states that I was triggered into. She would say something to provoke me and I would become reactive, defensive and get into survival state. It was fight, flight or freeze - and with her I would always fight. I would blow up, explode. My partner noticed she was the only person I ever talked to or treated that way. For the first 5 years of our relationship, we hadn't spent more than 14 nights away from each other - and he said he's never seen me as angry with anyone or in any situation as I would get with my mother.

I think my brain would actually shut off and shut down when this happens. My mind had created some sort of panic room and my conscious self would crawl in for protection. I would come out afterwards not really understanding what had happened. I felt so threatened by things she would say and just 'fly off the handle.'

Story 18:
Around the time I started writing this book I began having very angry and disturbed sleep. One night I dreamed that I was taking a secret trip back to my hometown. I vaguely remember my purpose as dropping things off at my parents house that my mother owned and I still had in my possession.

Oddly this was something I had actually done shortly before I had the dream. My dad had picked me up from the ferry and brought me into town to drop me off at my best friend's house to stay overnight. Before I left my house, I went around looking for items my mother had left at my house or loaned me. I needed them gone and took an opportunity to pass them off on my dad without having to actually step foot near the door of my house I had grown up in.

The dream carried on with my mother 'discovering' that I was back in town. She pursued me relentlessly. I remember in my dream being afraid during the chase. I ran through neighboring yards and climbed over fences to get her off my track. I was terrified of being discovered or encountering her. She hadn't actually laid eyes on me yet, but she was always close behind me. Always 'almost' catching me. The dream eventually morphed into a bird's eye view of my parents' bed. My adult brother was sleeping in the middle of my parents. My middle brother still lives with my parents in real life. No job, doesn't go to school. He just lives there.

At the end of the dream, the fear that woke me up came from dreaming that I was laying in a twin bed. My mother had crawled in beside me, even though there wasn't enough room for 2 people. She wrapped her arms around me and tried to hug or cuddle me. I began to struggle and push her away, trying to get her off the bed and away from me. But as I pushed...her arms stretched. Like silly putty. As I pushed on her face and chest and tried to get my knees up and in between us, her arms just stretched and stayed wrapped around me. They became cartoonish and a smile was developing on her face. My anxiety increased as I tried to fight to make her let go of me. I remember the colouring in this part of my dream. It was a dark room but the light parts were all shiny or glossy like when the moon hits something wet in the dark or an oil slick. I remember my mother's eyes looking like wet glass in the dark. She felt so sinister; she had an obvious maniacal pleasure in my inability to get away. I remember waking up terrified. I had an actual nightmare about trying to get away from my mother and her not letting me go.

Story 19:

I admit that I still imagine assaulting my mother. Sometimes. Not nearly as often as I used to. Sometimes a memory gets triggered. I go back to that place. I get sucked into a vivid recall. But I take the liberty of giving it a different ending. One where I get to physically express how angry and violent the emotions attached to the memory make me feel.

I remember the time my mother called a family meeting at the house we grew up in. It had to do with my father having PTSD and her insistence that we, as her children, were not supporting her in that struggle enough. She had spent a number of years during my early 20s spewing lectures to anyone that would listen about my father having extreme PTSD. It was all about his childhood trauma, him being triggered by his parents' death, and it all being stressed by his work as a firefighter. She took it upon herself to be the harbinger of his 'sickness.' She overloaded herself with research and advocacy for his self-awareness and recovery. She made herself the expert, the preacher, and the sole custodian of making sure everyone knew how damaged and broken my father was. At some point in my mid 20s she changed her tune to scolding us for not offering her enough support while having to 'live with him.' We as 'her family' and 'her children' were not doing 'enough' for her. It was a 'woe is me' harmony. I experienced multiple emails and phone calls over that time explaining how I wasn't doing enough for her, or my dad, during this extremely difficult time. She beckoned my brother and I to travel from our homes and families that were multiple hours of travel time away to sit and hear her scold us. My middle brother was still living in the house at about age 30. We sat around the dinner table after the meal was done. A rather anxious meal as my mother didn't approach the subject until we had all apprehensively picked through our plates, between awkward small talk.

I had spoken to my oldest brother before hand for advice on how to 'cope' with the situation ahead of us. His recommendation was to not engage. Tell her what she wants to hear. Ask her for clarification on what she wants. To not, for any reason, provoke the beast.

My mother spent a great length of time explaining where my father was at in his recovery. While he sat across from her at the table in silence. She continued on to explain our responsibilities as her children, to call and check in and be supportive and understanding of her and the amount of work and effort she was, and is, putting into helping my dad. She demanded that we begin believing her when she tells us things about our dad and how sick and fragile he is. She told us to stop questioning her about our dad's mental health because she knew better than we did. Because she has to live with it. Every. Day.

My oldest brother was calm, cool and collected. He asked simple questions about how we could do that. What changes she would like to see. I understood the game he had suggested, and the one I could see him playing. Placate her. Pacify her. I tried a few times...and struggled to not deviate. Every time I timidly began to ask a question, outside of the bounds he recommended, I had my mother's full eye contact and attention. I would look slightly past her to the other side of the table and could see my brother very gently shake his head. I could see his indication and I would derail my question.

There was a point in the family meeting that my father spoke. During some point my mother leaned across the table, pressing her index finger into the table in front of her and choking out an emotional "because you don't remember!"

Oddly this was before I had known what gaslighting was. But I knew was manipulation was. I also knew how unhealthy it was to keep telling someone how sick they were, when they are trying to recover. Which is exactly what I had gotten fed up with my mother for doing it to my dad. She felt her lack of support from me - because it was true. I had become so tired, so exhausted, so frustrated with continuing to hear her endless detailed descriptions of how broken, how damaged and how 'unrecovered' he was. I had actually set a boundary with her previous to this: She was no longer allowed to talk to me about my dad being sick. It was not a topic of conversation she was allowed to have with me.

Memory loss was one of the symptoms of extreme PTSD that she had christened him with. For a while I accepted this. I accepted her long list of ailments she had attached to my father. She brought her own downfall early on, as she encouraged us kids to support him and show him love. As I developed a closer relationship with my father during these years - I began to form my own assessment on how well he was or wasn't doing. Her lies and her game came unravelled from that point. Having one on one contact with my father, spending more time with him and finding inconsistencies with my mom's descriptions and diagnosis of him degan to discredit her. I could begin to question everything.

So as I watched my mother, shout at my father one more time "Because you don't remember!" I look back and wish I had reacted differently. I wish I hadn't succumbed to my brothers calculated escape plan. I wish I hadn't sat there, frozen.

**This story has been cut shorter than its original version, and I want anyone reading it to know why. The last paragraph originally went into a detailed description of a reimagined ending to this evening. A fantasy I had entertained at one point, where I mangle my mother.

The first person who came back to me with commentary and edits, before this book was published, asked why I had included this story. They asked, "Are you doing this to connect with a reader who may also have violent fantasies so that they don't feel alone? Not sure that's the message you want to deliver."

My friend is right. That is not the message I want to deliver to this world.

Writing out the darker ending to that story had a cathartic, but private place in time. But I don't need to release it into this world for others to experience.

The one I want to deliver is of mindfulness. The previous stories I share are examples of trauma with insight. They are to help other women gain confidence in the validity of their own memories of pain or discomfort. It is important to share stories of vulnerability to help others find courage. The entire point of this book is to encourage others to put out into the world what they hope to see and find around them. Love.

Cliff Notes

These are the cliff notes for those of you who need a refresher. Quick & to the point. Labels can be helpful but they can also be restrictive and cause holding patterns. Unless you are an accredited professional - be weary of labeling or diagnosing your mother. First - that's not your place. Second - at some point this will not be helpful any more, because; third - you should be focusing on who you want to be, which, if you have read this book, does not need to be determined by how you were raised.

Signs you have a Toxic Parent
1. You need to take care of them, make you responsible for their happiness
2. Their feelings come before yours; fail to provide affirmation or security
3. They control you using guilt or money
4. They refuse to let you grow up
5. They don't recognize your boundaries
6. The constantly undermine you or are overly critical or make 'jokes' about you
7. You're scared of them
8. They have high expectations with no acknowledgement of achievements
9. They envy you or compete with you
10. They never apologize or repair, blame you for their bad behavior

Types of Unloving Mothers (From Mother's Who Can't Love - by Susan Forward)
1. The severely narcissistic mother
2. The overly enmeshed mother
3. The control freak
4. Mothers who need mothering
5. Mothers who neglect, betray & batter

Narcissism: The hallmarks of **Narcissistic Personality** Disorder (**NPD**)
1. Grandiosity
2. A lack of empathy for other people
3. A need for admiration

People with this condition are frequently described as arrogant, self-centered, manipulative, and demanding (wikipedia)

**Also take a look at the extremely good list created by Karyl McBride in *Will I Ever Be Good Enough*, 2008

Expanded Traits of the Narcissist
1. Are highly reactive to criticism
2. Have low self-esteem
3. Lack of consideration for others' boundaries

4. Can be inordinately self-righteous and defensive
5. React to contrary viewpoints with anger or rage
6. Project onto others qualities, traits, and behaviors they can't—or won't—accept in themselves
7. Have poor interpersonal boundaries
8. An inability to communicate or work as part of a team
9. An inability to be truly vulnerable
10. Perfectionism

Add Sadism, Extreme Lack of Empathy for others and Proactive Manipulation for Malignant Narcissism

Traits of Narcissistic Abuse Survivors
1. Perfectionism
2. People-pleasing behavior
3. Low Self-esteem
4. No sense of self
5. Anxious mindset
6. Anger
7. Inability to express positive or negative emotions
8. Poor boundaries
9. Toxic shame
10. Trust issues
11. Cast off traits from the narcissist
12. Hopelessness

Gaslighting is a form of persistent manipulation and brainwashing that causes the victim to doubt her or himself, and to ultimately lose one's own sense of perception, identity, and self-worth. A gaslighter's statements and accusations are often based on deliberate falsehoods and calculated marginalization.

Tactics of a Gaslighter:
1. Frequent Lies and Exaggerations (Minimizing)
2. Discrediting their victim (Twisting and Reframing)
3. Rarely Admit Flaws and Are Highly Aggressive When Criticized
4. False Image Projection
5. Uses a mask of confidence, assertiveness and/or fake compassion
6. Rule Breaking and Boundary Violation
7. Emotional Invalidation and Coercion
8. Manipulation: The Use or Control of Others as an Extension of Oneself

Difference between Manipulation and Gaslighting

      Gaslighting is a form of manipulation which is aimed at undermining a target's connection to reality and trust in their own judgment. Manipulation itself is a term which covers a number of control tactics, gaslighting being one of them.

References for Beyond Damage

Chapter 1
11 laundry list for Adult Children of Alcoholics World Service Organization, The
Laundry List - 14 Traits of an Adult Child of an Alcoholic
www.adultchildren.org/literature/laundry-list/

Chapter 3
25 Wont you get lonely out there from the childrens' book *One Day Daddy*, by Frances
Thomas, Illustrated by Ross Collins; Copyright June 2001

Chapter 5
32 Each person is influenced by I was told this by my Uncle; repeatedly. I have no idea
where he got this from but through my own reading I found multiple sources and studies
reference this; including, but not limited to:
- *Breaking the Habit of Being Yourself*, Joe Dispenza; Copyright 2012
- Gene-Environment Interaction;
  https://developingchild.harvard.edu/science/deep-dives/gene-environment-
  interaction/
- Early literature & studies done by Robert Polmin exploring gene expression in
  twins

33 They often describe a feeling of a hole *The Emotionally Absent Mother*, Jasmin Lee
Cori, MS. LPC; Copyright April 2017, Chapter 5

Chapter 6
37 Psychological studies have determined that the 'voice inside our head' First
explored by Russian Psychologist Lev Vygotsky in the 1930s who proposed that private
speech is developed from social speech. Also see:
- *Development Psychology: Childhood & Adolescence*, David Shaffer, Katherine Kipp,
  Ninth Edition, Copyright January 2013, Chapter 10, 11 & 13
- Critical Inner Voice Defined, BestofYouTuday.com interview with Dr. Lisa
  Firestone, Ph. D, posted on https://www.psychalive.org/the-critical-inner-voice-
  defined/

Chapter 7
47 a story from eastern philosophy apparently has no known author; it is simply
regarded as an 'old Buddhist story'

85 Use the 70/20/10 Rule. The true origin of this term comes from a concept developed by Morgan McCall, Robert Eichinger and Michael Lombardo at the Center for Creative Leadership, whichproposes that on average, 70% of a person's learning at work is internal and experience-based, 20% comes from interacting with fellow employees and 10% is the result of formal training and reading. I have adopted the percentage breakdown of focus for my own tool.

Chapter 12
87 Munchausen Syndrome by proxy *"is a mental illness and a form of child abuse. The caretaker of a child, most often a mother, either makes up fake symptoms or causes real symptoms to make it look like the child is sick."*
https://medlineplus.gov/ency/article/001555.htm; Sept. 07 2017

88 Body Dysmorphic Disorder *is a mental health **disorder** in which you can't stop thinking about one or more perceived defects or flaws in your appearance — a flaw that appears minor or can't be seen by others.* https://www.mayoclinic.org/diseases-conditions/body-dysmorphic-disorder/symptoms-causes/syc-20353938 Oct. 29, 2019

89 bipolar/manic depressive 'spectrum.' *"The bipolar spectrum is a term used to refer to conditions that include not only bipolar disorder as traditionally defined (that is, clear episodes of mania or hypomania as well as depressive syndromes) but also other types of mental conditions that can involve depression or mood swings without manic or hypomanic episodes -- including some impulse control disorders, anxiety disorders, personality disorders, and forms of substance abuse."* https://www.webmd.com/bipolar-disorder/guide/bipolar-spectrum-categories#1 June 11, 2019

89 She was strongly against pharmaceuticals. I have to give my mother major credit for this. She is responsible for me dodging a major bullit with this. I have read the research that has come out over the years, discrediting SSRIs, and I will be forever thankful she discouraged me from getting on that train.

89 Her own research determined that anxiety and depression come from; I can give her half credit with this one. It was and still is true: research and studies show that depression is a common symptom among having poor sleep quality or lack of sleep, malnutrition and an absence of physical activity in one's life. But these are not an adequate substitute for lack of healthy emotional coping mechanisms, flared teenage hormones and a poor parent-child bond/attachment. It is also extremely dangerous to label or diagnose a teenager with a clinical and permanent disorder, especially when you are not a trained or certified professional.

91 imposter syndrome. *"First described by psychologists Suzanne Imes, PhD, and Pauline Rose Clance, PhD, in the 1970s, impostor phenomenon occurs among high achievers who are* *unable to internalize and accept their success. They often attribute their accomplishments to luck rather than to ability, and fear that others will eventually unmask them as a fraud."* https://www.apa.org/gradpsych/2013/11/fraud *Feel Like A Fraud?*; by Kirsten Weir, Nov. 2013

93 Next Level: Both Kara Loewentheil and Dr. Joe Dispenza are incredible in their field of offerings. Kara Loewentheil is the creator of Unf*ck Your Brain podcast, available on spotify. Find her at https://unfuckyourbrain.com/. Dr. Joe Dispenza is the author of *How to Evolve Your Brain & Breaking the Habit of Being Yourself*, was interviewed for What the Bleep Do We Know and now hosts a series on Gaia called Rewired; https://www.gaia.com/series/rewired

Chapter 15
117 some serious Stockholm bullshit is a condition which causes hostages to develop a psychological alliance with their captors during captivity. https://en.wikipedia.org/wiki/Stockholm_syndrome

118 Or rather - how your DNA operates and functions. This shit is mind blowing and everyone should know about it. *Breaking the Habit of Being Yourself*, Dr. Joe Dispenza, pg 77, copyright 2012

118 less than 5% of the diseases in the world are genetic. *Breaking the Habit of Being Yourself*, Dr. Joe Dispenza, pg 75, copyright 2012

www.ingramcontent.com/pod-product-compliance
Lightning Source LLC
Chambersburg PA
CBHW060250050426
42448CB00009B/1608